The S

Lost mines of the ancient miner
Covered well by the desert's hand.
Wealth found but not recorded,
The secret held by the sun and sand.

An old Sharps rifle stock all rotted;
How long in its grave will never be known.
Close by, bits of leather
Scattered over human bones.

Al Powell
Former special deputy
sheriff from
Walker, Arizona.

A grinning skull skeleton fingers
Greedily clutching the luring gold.
The sun and sand, the grinning skull
Know their secret will not be told.

Life against the sun and sand
Often leaves a grinning skull.
The desert plays a deadly game
Of winner takes it all.

On the horizon sets the burning sun
As far as the eye can see.
And it makes the sand roll like waves
Until the mountains are ships at sea.

The oasis seen; a desert trick,
Water holes dried to the core.
Maybe a rattler or a fall from a ledge
Left you still on the canyon floor.

Somewhere hidden a lost mine,
Each day the trail grows dimmer.
The sun and sand let the rattler sleep
In its decaying timber.

As the ancient miner fades forever
He need not record or remember.
The sun and sand left a grinning skull;
A lost mine and decaying timbers.

1

Acknowledgments

Tom Kollenborn—Curator, Superstition Mountain Historical Society

Robert K. Corbin—Attorney General of Arizona

Susie Sato—Librarian, Arizona Historical Foundation, Hayden Library, Arizona State University

Arizona Historical Society, Tucson, Arizona

University of Arizona Library

Photo Collection of the *Arizona Sheriff* magazine

Bucky Singleton—Senior Photographer, Motorola

Judge Flood—Justice of the Peace, Phoenix, former President of Dons Club (Deceased)

Theron Hardes—Commercial Artist

Holly McLean-Aldis—Editor

Lisa Owens—Technical Staff

The Gassler Family

Greg Davis—Superstition Mountain Historical Society, Director of Research and Acquisitions

Al Powell—Former Yavapai County Sheriff's Special Deputy, Walker, Arizona

Robin and Carol Fox—Design Directors

Trisha Kuhl—Superstition Photographer

THE CURSE OF THE
DUTCHMAN'S
GOLD

The true story of Arizona's
most cryptic mine.

By

HELEN CORBIN

Foxwest Publishing

THE CURSE OF THE DUTCHMAN'S GOLD

Copyright © 1990 by Helen Corbin

ISBN 1-879029-00-6

Graphics/Production: Robin Fox & Associates

10 9 8 7 6 5

Library of Congress Catalog Number: 90-083717

For information contact the Publisher:

Foxwest Publishing
2834 North 29th Street
Suite 1
Phoenix, AZ 85008

PUBLISHED IN THE UNITED STATES OF AMERICA

To Bob and Tom . . .
the treasure was in the seeking.

Table of Documents, Maps and Photographs

Table of Contents

Dedication

From the Author

Special Section (center insert)
Contains the Ortiz Map, the Ortiz Letter, Tom
Kollenborn's Map, Peralta Locator Map, the
Fish Treasure Map and the Dutchman Map

From the Author

The mysterious Superstition Mountains of Arizona hold the secret to one of the richest gold mines ever found. It has not been actively worked since the 1800s when Jacob Waltz, a German immigrant known as the Dutchman, mined it.

In 1984, Datapol, an Arizona computer research firm, uncovered an interesting fact regarding incoming tourists. Highest on their list of priorities were the Grand Canyon and the Lost Dutchman Mine, in that order.

According to the German government's information bureau, movies shown on the subject resulted in so many calls to the television stations that to quell interest the bureau issued a statement that the mine had been found.

The priest in the town of Wurttemberg, where Jacob was born, said he had so many inquiries regarding the man and his family that it became necessary to refuse release of information to anyone.

Every year thousands of people hike over the Dons Club trails just to see the infamous land known as the Superstition Mountain Range.

For almost 200 years interest in that particular mine has lured untold numbers to search for it. Chronologically they include: the Indians, Spanish, Mexicans, prospectors, soldiers, and finally, treasure hunters—many of whom died in the process.

The Superstitions—Hell's backyard—were home to the Apaches. Possession of the yellow metal meant nothing to the savages; they considered it a trinket and freely gave it to Spanish soldiers. Then, greed from ruthless conquerors forced astute medicine men to decree the wrath of the gods on those who told of its whereabouts. That dictum started a war which lasted well into the 1900s.

Protection of their secret turned the Apaches into fierce adversaries. Their methods of torture defied comparison. On occa-

9

sion a battered body would be found on the trail, an ominous warning to those who dared to follow. Usually the individual's eyes were gouged out and the scalp was missing. Sometimes the bodies were staked over an ant hill or propped into a standing position on sharp sticks driven there while the tormented soul was still alive. Those haunting reminders, told and retold, caused frightened settlers, who became entrapped, to kill family members rather than allow them to be taken prisoner.

One woman, who was later traded back to the Army, told of being marched barefooted for 50 miles while tied behind the horses of her Indian captors. After losing her little sister to exposure and infection, she was forced to walk through glowing, hot mesquite beds while being prodded with burning sticks by vicious squaws and children. She commented that, "Death would have been sweeter." Unable to return to the white man's world, she was later committed to an asylum.

Being tortured wasn't the only threat. Treasure seekers who became delirious often died of thirst in the scorching 125-degree heat where water is more precious than gold. And the forbidding desert terrain contained rattlesnakes and gila monsters whose bite resulted in long, painful deaths. Riddled with impassable crags, an eager climber might slip, only to fall hundreds of feet into shadowy, unforgiving depths where animals eventually stripped away their dead flesh. Then there was the danger of man. Some 68 unexplained deaths have been recorded in that mountain range since the turn of the century. A few were suicides; some accidental, but most of those occurred because of a hunch that bonanza was near; futile murders over gold which the earth still clutches tenaciously.

No records exist which would describe the numbers of Mexicans, Spanish or Indians who moved with stealth through those treacherous canyons. History recorded the battles. Later, however, there would be at least 11 prospectors destined to learn of the mine's secret location. Once they located the gold, their lives were ended. (That evidence will be produced in this text.)

Is the mine cursed? It seems so—only Jacob Waltz, for whom

the mine is named, survived it. Perhaps the Dutchman was the figure selected by the fates to be the catalyst for mystery, intrigue and sardonic lure.

Curiosity about the mine is worldwide, thereby raising a multitude of theories. Cynics argue that there isn't a mine and Jacob is a myth. Others are confident the German high-graded ore from some working Arizona gold strike, of which there were many in his day. Still others deduce Jacob found a cache hidden by the Spanish. There are also long-standing rumors of a chimney of gold which has been worked out. Many books state unequivocally that the mine has already been found and the gold claimed. Some stories say Jacob murdered two Mexican peons to get the mine. And, of course, there is the Peralta land grant theory which assumes Jacob was given the rights to the mine for having saved the life of one of their sons. Whatever theory is correct, Jacob's gold, last found in May of 1985 and claiming another victim, is worth $1,600,000 to the ton on today's market.

And—what of the man himself? Waltz has been labeled a cold-blooded murderer, a womanizer, a thief, a drunkard, a loner and by contrast: a kind, gentle, industrious teetotaler and, more than once, a good friend.

To set the story straight, Jacob's gold appears in full color on the cover of this book photographed for the first time by Motorola's head photographer, Bucky Singleton. Explanations of the charges against Waltz will be given with as much proof as possible considering the lapse of nearly 100 years since his October 1891 death. To complete this task, records were garnered from the files of Tom Kollenborn, the leading authority on the Lost Dutchman mine, and his partner Bob Corbin.

In order to solve the puzzle, undeniable documents, photographs and news clippings will be presented. They are the result of Kollenborn's 44-year search for the truth and from never-before-published notes of three men.

Kollenborn, curator of the Superstition Mountain Historical Society, geologist and teacher, spends all of his weekends atop his horse, Crow, wending his way through the labyrinth of trails.

11

His fascination with the mountains, their lore and inhabitants brought him into the range as a young man after hearing the story from his mining engineer father.

Before college, Kollenborn punched cows at the Barkley Ranch, formerly known as Bark's Ranch, one of the main points of interest in this story. All of the clues are included within these pages plus Tom's map which took him over three decades to catalog. The map (the only one of its kind) marks every point mentioned in the book and some which are only alluded to.

The reader also will be privy to excerpts from the notes of three men who spent most of their lifetimes searching for the mine. The first of them, Jim Bark, knew Jacob Waltz.

Bark owned the ranch within those perimeters the mine is supposed to be located. He enjoyed prominence as a civic leader in Arizona's territorial days and ran for the first legislature. Later, besides searching for the mine with his friend and confidant, newsman Sims Ely, he kept copious notes on the area's happenings.

Brownie Holmes, the second contributor, died in 1980. It was Brownie's father, Dick Holmes, who was with Jacob as he lay dying. Holmes laid claim to the ore under Jacob's deathbed and later gave the world the impression that it had been a bequest. (The photograph of that gold appears on the cover.)

Walter Gassler is the third man and the latest victim. His story appears in the final chapter. Walter anguished over the gold from 1932 until his death in May of 1985 when the curse claimed him.

There are two other prominent figures in this scenario. The pair were probably Waltz's only close friends in his last days. They were a mulatto woman named Julia E. Thomas, who is also referred to as Helena, and her adopted son, a Caucasian boy of German extraction named Rhinehart (Reiney) Petrasch.

The Dutchman owned a small farm near the Salt River where he had been caught in a record flood which bore down on Phoenix in February of 1891. Reiney, having been sent to fetch the old prospector, found him crouched atop his bed, shivering and wet. Julia and Reiney moved him to a one-room adobe behind her home. Later, Jacob contracted pneumonia from which he never recovered.

It was during this period the German decided to tell his friends where the mine was. The knowledge of it ruined the remainder of their lives and the lives of Reiney's only living relatives—his father and brothers. It also triggered an ongoing feud between the Holmes and Petrasch factions of Dutchman hunters. The camps remain divided. That fact adds intrigue to the tale and helps explain the discrepancies which occur throughout the story.

Neither Julia nor Reiney ever found the mine and their lives ended tragically.

Sims Ely, the last in this cast of characters, arrived in Phoenix shortly after the Dutchman's death. He was to survive his friend, Bark, and would in his declining years write a book titled, *The Lost Dutchman Mine*. It is now out of print.

Deciphering the puzzle is accomplished by comparing the notes and the interviews which Ely had with Julia, with Bark's constant interrogation of Reiney and the notes of Brownie Holmes revealed after the latter's death in 1980. Of course, Brownie's notes are based on what his father told him about the event. All of these sources have been printed verbatim.

Conclusions are, after all, up to the reader but evidence herein should, for once and for all time, lay to rest the doubts as to who and what Jacob was, whether or not there is a mine, if it was as rich as they claimed, and if the mine can be found again.

Contained within these pages and documents lies the secret to the mine's location. Searching for it is only for the hardy and the fearless, or for those who are dedicated to burning the midnight oil, poring over maps and enjoying a vicarious adventure through reading about it.

Chapter 1

When Death Finally Came

Saturday night in an early Western cowtown was always a raucous affair and Phoenix was no exception. But by Sunday's pre-dawn the dust from the cowboys' horses usually had settled and the new light of day, not quite over the giant Superstition Mountains 50 miles to the east, would soon be spewing warm rays.

Thankfully summer had faded. There never was much of a breeze but the desert seemed cool and invited the sounds of birds and the cock crowing a new day. A mangy dog out behind the saloon barked his hope for a few scraps from the Chinaman cleaning out the kitchen.

Inside the Faro game had ended. Bearded, soiled players waited ignoring two drunks sprawled on the floor near the bar. This wasn't an ordinary Sunday in October of 1891. Down the street, out behind Julia Thomas' home in an adobe hut, lay a dying man whose feverish lips held the greatest secret in the West. All the previous night the crowd in the bar had talked of nothing else. Jacob Waltz's death wouldn't bring remorse; instead, they were like vultures—expectant and hungry for the knowledge of the location of the old man's mine.

The adobe was cool. Julia brushed a weary hand across Jacob's damp hair. His labored breaths were harder now and panic gripped her. She wished Reiney were there. "Where is that boy?

He would pick tonight to disappear. I need someone here while I get the doctor," she thought. Suddenly she could wait no longer. Jacob was the color of his beard, sickening white. In all of the eight months since the flood when he contracted pneumonia he had never been this bad. Her worst fears were being realized. Jacob was dying. Leaping up from the chair beside his wooden bunk, she rushed out into the yard toward her home. As she appeared in the doorway, she cried out, "Come quick! Jacob Waltz is almost dead. I've got to get the doctor."

Julia's voice reached two cowboys lurking near the front who reacted by racing inside just as she hurried up the street.

(From all the accounts garnered through later interviews, this is what took place.)

Dick Holmes was just outside the house waiting with another man who died shortly thereafter. Holmes' presence there was no accident. Remember, it was probably 4:30 A.M. Dick had been trailing Jacob trying to learn the location of his mine for a long time; he even had an accomplice. But the world wouldn't learn of his chicanery until 1983 when his son, Brownie, died and Dick's story came to light through Brownie's notes.

The following account in Brownie's own words explains how Dick Holmes learned of Jacob's mine and what then transpired.

(Please remember that all notes in this text are reprinted exactly as the originals appear.)

Brownie's Notes

The "Bloody Basin" country lies approximately seventy miles north of Phoenix. It is very sparingly settled country in spite of the fact that it is excellent range land. It was here that my grandfather and his son, my father, established their horse and cattle ranch about the year 1882. The ranch house was erected on the bank of a creek which was fed from several springs. The older maps still show this small creek as Holmes Creek. Although the ranch prospered from the beginning, there were times when it did not require the close attention of both men. As a consequence, Grandfather Holmes would spend considerable time prospecting, as did a number of ranchers in those

ARIZONA DAILY GAZETTE
JUNE—4, 1892 p. 4 d. 2
Cave Creek Onyx.

R. J. Holmes came in from Cave Creek onyx mines m... day, where he has seventeen men a' v k taking out stone for shipment. ...

T. ... ... is widening with ... ... of development and the ... becoming more solid, and is ...ing out in large blocks. One piece brought in this week by Coyle's teams weighed over 6,000 pounds, and is of a pretty greenish cast.

Two carloads will be shipped from Phoenix to-day.

First sentence of the Arizona Daily Gazette article dated 1892 is documented proof that R. J. (Dick) Holmes lived.

days. Sometimes he would be away from home for several weeks and father would remain alone at the ranch. In the winter of 1884, grandfather departed for the hills to be gone for a period of several weeks. Father was the type of a man that enjoyed the companionship of a fellow being and after spending several days and nights without having seen any sort of humanity, not even a friendly Indian, he was overjoyed one cold winter evening when John Phipps, a prospector, rode up to the ranch and called a friendly "Hello." Mr. Phipps was a genial old fellow about sixty years of age, but carried himself gracefully in spite of his advancing years. It was not the first time that father had met the old gentleman for he was in the habit of stopping at various ranches throughout the country on his frequent journeys to and fro from the hills to the south. On this particular evening, the area was being visited by one of its regular and sometimes rather severe winter rains. The cold, biting wind whipped unmercifully down the canyon from the north. The accompanying rain, driving in sheets, seemed to chill to the bone. Father assisted the old man in getting his outfit sheltered. He then built a roaring fire and, after placing a large tub under a leak in the roof, set to making the visitor comfortable. They talked about things in general as father prepared the evening meal. He inquired about people they both knew and wondered what had become of so and so. After

17

the supper, a large sack of black walnuts was brought forth. These had been gathered the previous fall from the many trees in the "Basin" country. The old man's clothes were dry before long and as the two were now feeling comfortable in the cozy cabin. With wind howling outside and the rain whipping itself against the roof in occassional torrents, they resumed their conversation. "Dick!" Mr. Phipps exclaimed suddenly, as if an inspiration to leave the cabin right then and there had come over him, "What would you say if I told you that I could take you to a place where you could fill the tub with pure gold?" Father gazed at him quizically for a moment and with a smile replied: "I would say, let's go at once." He had sudden bursts of enthusiasm before coming from the mouths of old prospectors who had just found the thing they had been searching for these many years. Even his own father had come home on many an occassion with a mere handful of pay-dirt declaring there was plenty more where that came from. Somehow, they did not go back to the place where the rich find had been made, for in the meantime, someone had told them of another rich strike in another direction. And so it was with all prospectors. Phipps continued on with his remarkable story: "In the big rough mountains south of the Salt River is a very rich mine. Dick, an old German from Phoenix is working it secretly. I have watched the mine for three or four years. . . ." Here father interrupted with, "Who is this old German, John. . .?" "His name is Wolz—Jacob Wolz" the old fellow replied. "And his is an ornery old devil too. Why, he's killed a dozen men, I suppose—the only time I've had the nerve to go into the diggins is when I know darn well he's out of the hills. I built a small rock shelter in a cliff high above the floor of the canyon where I would be protected from the weather and other danger. When I was sure that Wolz was not in the mountains, I would dig out some gold and get out of there." "How much gold do you think is in the mine, John," father asked. "Plenty," the old prospector replied. "That's the richest vein of ore I've ever seen. Why, Dick, you can take out a thousand dollars a day easy." "How long have you been watching the old Dutchman?" "For several years now, but I haven't been in there for a year or so though." "Why not?" father asked. The old fellow laughed and remained silent for a moment. "You see, it is like this," he exclaimed. "I thought the old fellow was out of the hills, so I began robbing the mine. I had just finished for the day and was going to my hideout on the side of the canyon to rest, I looked down the canyon and by God, there he was coming back." The old fellow shuddered as though a sudden chill had gripped him. "You know, Dick," he continued, "I'm not a coward, by God, I don't want another experience like that one. The way that old German acted when he saw that someone had disturbed his mine—man, that was terrible. "How did he act?" father inquired. "He began looking for tracks, and knowing if he were able to trail me, he would shoot, I kept hid and when night came I sure got away from there fast." "Why don't you locate the mine and record it?" father asked. "Not me" old John replied. "That old Dutchman has killed many a man, and he'd kill me in a minute when he found out I located the thing. Nope, I'm getting old, but I've still got a right mind. Dick, by God, I'm afraid of him and I'm not going back until I know damn well he's six feet under the ground." "Well, I'm not afraid of him," father declared emphatically. "If you show me where this mine is, I'll locate the damn thing." He was yet to learn the ruthless and vicious character of Jacob Wolz. His explosive declaration seemed to startle old John for a moment. Then he looked father straight in the eye and said "Dick, the German is nearly eighty years old and he won't last much longer. When he dies, I'll take you in as a partner and we will locate the thing. I guess I've already said too much." He closed up like a clam. Try as he would, father could not get any more information out of John Phipps regarding a certain gold deposit, which was destined to become the most talked of mine, real or imaginary, in the history of the West. A mine which, during the passing years, had been responsible for the death of at least one man and which my father sent on many disappointing trips into the Superstitions. And later myself, his son, on the same quest. Always hoping, always believing it was just over the next hill. Phipps remained with father for two weeks, during which time he remained, or rather maintained intense silence every time father brought up the subject of the mine of the Super-

Photograph taken of Jacob Waltz after his arrival in New York.

stitions. He was a congenial soul enough as he helped with the ranch chores and discussed many subjects in general, but as far as the old German's mine was concerned, he was through. After leaving the ranch, he made his way into the Mazatzal Mountains, a wild and remote range, far to the east of the Basin. He spent the rest of the winter alone prospecting here and there, but never discovering anything except an occassional piece of rock that disclosed some few colors when panned. As spring came on, he joined a bunch of cattlemen and assisted in their spring roundup. The cowboys established their camp one evening on the creek and Phipps in his usual industrious manner, set about digging the sand from the sides of a deep water hole when it began to cave in upon him. He fought frantically to disengage himself from the clutches of the wet sand which had now covered him up to the waist. His cries for help attracted the attention of the cowboys, and they immediately rushed to his rescue. But before they could reach the unfortunate man, another avalance of sand fell on him and covered him to his shoulders. He was quick to realize the terrible predicament of being almost completely submerged in the deadly wet sand and becoming almost to the point of hysterics, offered a lavish reward for his immediate rescue. He told the startled cowboys, in a gasping breath that he would take them to the richest gold mine in the world—he would show them more gold than they could carry out—if they would only hurry and get him out of the hole, which was slowly and surely claiming him as a victim. The cowboys were momentarily stunned at the impending fate of the aged prospector and, without even considering the promised reward, rushed to their saddles for ropes with which to pull him out of the hole. Before they could get back to render aid another avalanche occurred and he was smothered in several feet of sand. There in the bottom of the water hole, high in the Mazatals with the promise of gold on his lips, they left his body buried in a living grave dug by nature and filled by the hand of Providence; and with him was buried a secret known now to only one man living—old Jacob Wolz. The cowboys conducted a thorough search through his personal effects for some clue, which might disclose the whereabouts of relatives. They were unsuccessful in their quest for information as there was not a scrap of paper in his belongings. The search revealed, among other things, however, two one-pound baking powder cans that were filled with gold. Father made frequent trips to Phoenix during the five years following the death of Phipps. It was during this five-year period that my father met my mother and they were married in 1891. Shortly after his marriage he disposed of his "Bloody Basin" holdings and moved to this thriving little western town, which even then was well on its way to become one of the most progressive and metropolitan cities in the inland southwest. About the year 1888 he met an old German who was called "Old Snow" by the people of Phoenix. They struck up a friendship and, after having made several inquiries regarding the old man, was surprised to learn that he was Jacob Wolz. Father was very discreet in his conversations with the old German in that he never mentioned anything whatsoever regarding the mine in the Superstitions. He felt that the old man would take the secret to the grave, and inasmuch as the sole possessor of the fabulous deposit of ore was getting very old, he began to watch and wait for an opportunity to learn more vital bits of information. Old Jake would disappear at the first sign of winter and the rumors were generally circulated around the town that he was in possession of a gold mine from which he got gold necessary to purchase several choice pieces of property in and adjoining Phoenix. He always had plenty of money on his person and those of a later day said that he often drank heavily, gambled freely, and boasted of his rich mine in the Superstitions. According to statements made by my father and others who were fairly close to him, he was not of that disposition. On the contrary, he was very secretive and took extraordinary pains to guard his every movement. For weeks before disappearing into the mountains, small quantities of food stuff were purchased over a period of weeks before the old man departed for the mountains. This he accumulated with the secure feeling that he was unnoticed by the curious inhabitants. His one failing, which was the cause of a sometimes close watch being kept on him, was that he became somewhat over-enthusiastic just before departure and made many purchases in the course of two or three days. After having secured a sufficient amount to last him throughout the winter months, he would make his departure under cover of darkness and would often approach the mountains by a circuitous route. Sometimes he would camp for several days by the side of some remote water hole and watch diligently for a possible follower. My father began to notice the old man's activities and he became extremely interested in the various rumors circulating around the community regarding his exploits. His memory carried him back to that cold winter night when the prospector, Phipps, told him he could take him to a place where he could fill a tub with pure gold. He also recalled the tragic incident of the water hole cave-in, when Phipps became frantic and offered to take the cowboys to the richest gold mine in the world. Came a day when a friend, whose name was McFall, met father on the street. They talked for a few moments about things in general and nothing in particular, when Jacob Wolz approached them with several bundles in his arms. The old man was the first to speak. "How do you do, gentlemen?" he spoke in a broken drawl. "Fine," father and McFall replied. "And how are you these days?" father asked. The old man mumbled something about the weather and continued on his way. He showed every indication of having been an exceptional man in his early days. His broad shoulders were bowed somewhat and his gait was slower perhaps than the average man, but he carried his nearly eighty years remarkably well. As he turned a corner on his way to his home, McFall turned to father and said; "Dick, let's you and I follow Wolz into the mountains. He's not going to last much longer, and we might as well try to locate his mine before it's too late." "It's two-a-go, Mac," father said. "We'll have to keep a continual watch on him day and night from now on," McFall answered. "If you'll watch him during the day, I'll keep him covered at night." "Fine," came back father, "I'll start right away and watch him until dark then you carry on where I leave off." McFall looked disconsolate for a moment and then said, "Dick, I'm not too much of a hand at trailing and I think I might do more harm than good in following the old man, and it would be fatal if we were caught in the act." To this father agreed. "I've had considerable experience, Mac, and if you'll just keep me posted as to his time of leaving I'll do the rest." Father watched the old man closely from morning till night. The two men seldom spoke now, as McFall would take up his duties when darkness came on. They would merely pass one another on the street and nod their heads in recognition. It was almost two o'clock one morning when father was awakened with a knock on the door of his home. "Dick, wake up—it's me, McFall."

Father dressed hurriedly and opened the door to let him inside. He could see by the excitement on his friend's face that the Dutchman had departed. "What's up?" he inquired. "Jake Wolz has left," McFall answered. "Gone about an hour." "Which direction did he go?" "Southeast towards the river," said McFall. "Did you trail him?" "Yes, about two miles. Once he stopped and I thought he had seen me. For God's sake be careful, Dick." "Just where did you leave him?" "Right where the old wagon road forks. He took the one to the left." "Good," father replied. "I'll have pretty good sailing at the start anyway." Father grabbed up some food, biscuits, bacon and some jerky then, hastily placing this in a sack, he mounted his horse and departed into the night. He didn't travel along the road, but kept more out in the desert, the better to conceal the sound of the horse's hoof beats. Arriving at the spot where McFall had last observed the old German, he dismounted and hid the horse in the bushes or thicket. He then started off on foot and, after trailing the pack mules for a couple of miles, returned to his mount and rode to that spot, repeating the maneuver of the ride and the method of trailing. That is riding a ways and then walking on foot to a point about two miles distant, then returning to the horse and riding again. This method of trailing considerably lessens the danger of detection. *The first night after his departure from Phoenix, Wolz camped on the Verde River about two miles north of the place where Granite Reef diversion dam now is.* He unpacked his mules and hobbled them and then set about preparing an evening meal. As night came on the winter cold became more intense. Father could not enjoy the comforting warmth of a campfire and he envied the old German whose fire was blazing and crackling merrily. He had crawled up to within a hundred yards of Wolz's camp, keeping the old man under constant observation until his arms and legs became numb from cold. He then retreated to his makeshift camp and made preparations for a long, hard uncomfortable night without having had the satisfaction of an evening meal. Jake Wolz was up early the next morning. Father had spent a very uncomfortable night and was wide awake, when shortly before dawn he observed a long column of smoke climbing heavenward, which signified the old German was preparing morning meal. He waited for nearly an hour after having first observed the smoke before venturing forth to note the direction the old man was taking in crossing the river. The brush was thick along the river, and he had very little difficulty in ascertaining the whereabouts of Wolz without being seen. The trail crossed the river at an angle, and father could see the faint outline of the pursued man and his mules. Just as they were disappearing in an easterly direction from the previous night's camp. Father munched his hard biscuits and jerky as he traveled afoot and on horseback through the thick cottonwood and mesquite of the Verde bottom. On two or three occassions he came within sighting distance of the German and always when this occurred he would hold back to allow Wolz to gain distance. *The trail led to Cottonwood Wash and as evening approached, Wolz made his camp at Agua Escondido (Spanish for Hidden Water),* so named because this spring is hidden from view. It was a beautiful spot with cottonwood and sycamore trees lined up on either side of the small outlet of the spring, an ideal place for a campground, even in those days of long ago. Once again an uncomfortable night, spent without campfire. However, like most of the hardy pioneers of those days he took the distressing situation as a mere matter of a day's work and thought lightly of it. Early the next morning the pursuer and the pursued wound their way slowly towards *the Salt River, which was crossed a short distance below where Mormon Flats Dam now stands. Thence to Tortilla Creek to Tortilla Spring,* where Wolz made preparation for his third night's camp. *This point is now less than fifty yards east of Tortilla Creek by the famous Apache Trail Highway.* They were now in the northern part of the Superstition Mountains. Father used every precaution to prevent possible detection after crossing the Salt River. He went on foot to a spot near the spring and then crawled on his hands and knees through the dense brush and cactus for several hundred yards, arriving at a point about a hundred yards from the German's camp, he observed a startling spectacle, one which would make a brave man experience cold chills up and down his spinal column. There sitting on a pile of rock, with his rifle in his hands ready for action, and looking the way he had come, sat Jacob Wolz. There was a ferocious scowl on his face which plainly disclosed the fact that there was murder in his heart, and father, realizing that the jig was up so to say, backed cautiously out of the brush. There was no sense or reason in pursuing Wolz any further now that he was distinctly on the defensive. To continue the old man's trailing would mean that one of them would not come back. Father would not think of killing the old man. In the first place, Wolz had never injured him in any way. As a matter of fact, he felt more kindly towards father than he did towards most of his acquaintances and also, if it became necessary to fight it out as they would surely do if he trailed further, and if the old man should be killed—right then and there would go the secret of the mine. Father was thinking of all of this as he returned to his horse, about a mile or so distant from the spring camp. It was possible, he thought, that the German had discovered that he was being followed, but it was not probable that he had learned the identity of who was trailing him. Later father found out he was wrong in his assumption. The following spring Wolz returned to Phoenix and, meeting father on the street one day, said in a slow accented drawl, "Dick, I have something to say to you." "Surely, Mr. Wolz," he returned guiltily. There was never the least inkling in the old man's speech or actions that would indicate any ill feeling on his part and father was very much surprised when he said. "You tried to follow me into the mountains, but don't ever do it again, because the next time, I will surely kill you. I like you Dick, and I don't want to harm you, but remember what I have said." With that, the old man continued on his way, leaving father there with the feeling that he was about the lowest creature in the world. He would rather have had the old man come to him storming and cussing, for then he would have put up an argument and would have had the satisfaction of holding his own. But to be talked to like a little bad boy who had done some mischievous trick of not much consequence hurt his pride considerably. He was a capable tracker and he knew it, as constant work on the range had taught him this. He realized the old German was unusually shrewd in detecting the fact that he was being watched and trailed by an expert in the game. Needless to say, father did not follow him on any subsequent trips. And he realized now what a ruthless killer the Dutchman was and doubted his wisdom in following him in the first place. Wolz made his last trip to the mine in the winter of 1891-2. History will tell you that it was one of the worst storm-ridden winters ever experienced in the southern part of Arizona. Wolz was working his mine when the storm broke, and catching cold, he packed part of his ore and came to Phoenix. By the time he arrived he was a very sick man. He was put to bed and attended by an old Cuban Negress. Despite her efforts, he gradually became worse and pneumonia developed. Realizing that his time on earth was growing short, he called her to his bedside and told her that he was going to die and that he wished to give directions to his mine. Mrs. Thomas became very excited and rushed from the house to obtain help. My father and a friend named Gideon Roberts, a much older man than my father, were the first people she met. She told them of the old German's condition. Father sent her for a doctor and he and Roberts hastened to the bedside of the stricken man. When they arrived at Wolz's home he told them to sit down and addressing my father said, "Dick, my time is short and I want to give you the directions to my mine." (Please remember that Wolz spoke broken English and was not familiar with the entire Superstition Range. He had no reason to explore them. He already had pay dirt. Even today there are many unnamed canyons and hills within the range and at the time of his death there were less than half a dozen named places. Therefore his directions were limited to the Government Trail and marker. When Mrs. Thomas returned with the doctor Wolz had passed away. But not before he had told father and Roberts one of the most fantastic stories ever told about a hidden gold deposit in the history of the West.)

If the reader will grant this researcher license this seems a good time to pause to discuss some pertinent facts.

John Phipps stated, "I built a small rock shelter in a cliff high above the floor of the canyon where I would be protected from the weather and other danger. When I was sure that Wolz (sic) was not in the mountains, I would dig out some gold and get out of there." Later, on that same page, John said in answer to

Dick's question as to why he didn't continue to dig out gold. "I thought the old fellow was out of the hills, so I began robbing the mine. I had just finished for the day and was going to my hideout on the side of the canyon to rest, I looked down the canyon and my God, there he was coming back."

Some might disagree, but those words indicate that the mine and the hideout were high up. In that terrain sighting the German returning would require height. It also seems reasonable to assume that Phipps would have built his hideaway close to the mine so that he could escape easily and hide if and when he felt threatened.

The description of Jacob's trek to the mine when Holmes was trailing him is italicized for the treasure hunter, but one must realize it is later discussed that the German knew he was being followed. Therefore, we might suppose that he didn't take his natural route or might have changed course after he noticed his trackers.

Now, there is one glaring discrepancy in this part of Brownie's notes. He states that Wolz (sic) made his last trip to the mine in the winter of 1891 to 1892. It is a recorded fact that Jacob died October 25, 1891. It might not be worth mentioning except for the rest of that story. Brownie's father supposedly told him that Jacob was caught in the Superstitions at his mine in a winter storm which was so bad it caused the old man to become ill and return to Phoenix. Of course, you will see this story differs considerably with Bark's notes and Ely's account of how Jacob came to be at the adobe with the negro woman and her boy.

Much later it became an accepted fact that Jacob Waltz told Dick Holmes where the mine was while Julia went for the doctor. Now, let's examine that statement.

Brownie admits in his notes that his father and another man had been trailing the Dutchman in an effort to locate the mine and that Jacob had said he would kill them if they tried it again. Why then would this man suddenly want to tell them the secret? For eight long months Julia and Reiney had nursed an ailing, lonely old man. What kind of person in his last moments on earth would forget such kindness? What is possible, if the German was lucid at the last moment, however, is that he decided to leave this world with a smile on his face. Admittedly, Jacob was clever and smart. Perhaps, realizing that his moments were short and facing an old enemy, Jacob Waltz told Dick Holmes a story which sounded plausible. Just enough truth to send him on a wild goose chase which would last for two generations. Then, having outwitted his tormentors, he could die happy. He had had eight months to tell his friends where to look and probably believed he had done all that he could under the circumstances. And, if the Indian legends were correct, no one was supposed to find the mine anyway.

On the other hand, if Jacob was delirious, consider his accent and labored breathing; how accurate could any description have been?

Furthermore, the gold which was supposed to be hidden under the bed at the time of his death was missing the next evening after the funeral.

Dick had very rich ore assayed at Goldman's store early in 1892. The specimens which were assayed came to $20.64 an ounce. At 5,500 ounces to the ton that would mean the gold was worth $110,000 a ton in the late 1800s.

The fact is that Dick Holmes spent the remainder of his life searching for the Dutchman's mine—he died without finding it. His son, Brownie, imbibed with the lore, spent all of his life doing the same without success.

Brownie didn't die until 1980 after a long illness during which he accrued enormous medical bills. Just before his death they were all paid.

At the same time a successful businessman from Mesa, Arizona, who was also a close personal friend of Brownie's, came into possession of valuable gold ore; a matchbox made of slabbed gold ore created by a San Francisco jeweler in the 1900s, a pair of gold cuff links from the same ore and an assay report made out to Dick Holmes. On today's market, that ore would assay out at $1,600,000 to the ton. The report which was made in 1892 bore the name of Goldman's store in Phoenix.

The same businessman, preferring to remain anonymous for obvious reasons, also showed Tom Kollenborn and Bob Corbin a letter from the University of Arizona's School of Mines which stated that said ore "Came from no known Arizona mine." (An affidavit to that effect begins on page 233.) For the uninitiated it is a pure and simple fact that country rock surrounding mineral in place is readily identifiable to the geographic location where it was found. A good assayer can usually name the mine offhand and often, if he is very experienced, can identify the range and place.

This conclusive bit of evidence lays to rest once and for all time the theory that Jacob was high-grading ore from some working gold mine.

And, since Brownie Holmes died broke, it is fair to assume Dick Holmes passed the treasure on to his son as a legacy.

The fact that neither man ever located the mine is well known. In the last chapter of Brownie's notes he admits that the gold came from the candlebox under Jacob's bed as he lay dying. Whether it was a gift or a theft there is no one left to say.

Whatever the facts, having a priceless small treasure in his possession only whetted Dick's appetite for more gold. That obsession consumed the father and son all of their lives.

Tom Kollenborn, an educated and precise man, interviewed Brownie many times before his death. He was satisfied beyond a doubt that his subject was mentally alert. Holmes claimed the ore was a gift from a dying man.

Jacob Waltz died at 6 A.M. October 25, 1891. His obituary notices from two local newspapers follow. By 10 A.M. he was buried in the old city cemetery which is two blocks from the Arizona State Capitol. (Because of the heat and the fact that there were no embalming facilities, bodies were disposed of immediately.)

The marker on Jacob's grave has been destroyed by vandals and only a handful of stalwarts know its whereabouts. During 1984 a group was formed to raise funds to have a headstone cut

The articles above are copies of the obituary notices from the *Phoenix Daily Herald* and the *Arizona Daily Gazette* pertaining to Jacob Waltz's death, dated 1891.

for the Dutchman's grave—the man who gave Arizona its most famous legend.

* * *

At this point, let's pause to review the first mystery in this bizarre tale.

Julia told Sims when she and Reiney returned from the cemetery that they were busy with mundane chores and did not look for the gold until it was dark. The candlebox was still there, but the gold was gone. This fact certainly evoked sympathy for the woman who had done so much for the dying old prospector.

There is much proof that Dick Holmes took rich gold to the assay office to sell early in 1892. It also is a fact that Dick Holmes gave gold to his son. Later, a story went around that Dick stole the gold while Julia went for the doctor. Dick's son Brownie would go to his grave claiming the Dutchman gave it to him.

In Jim Bark's notes, which occur later in the book, Reiney reported saying that Julia did not go to the funeral. She claimed she was too upset by the old man's death.

Julia said she and Reiney went to the funeral.

Someone didn't tell the truth and that matter later would divide Dutchman hunters into two camps: the Petrasch followers and the Holmes followers. Both groups are dedicated to their beliefs and never the twain shall meet.

Tom Kollenborn theorizes that Julia reclaimed the gold while Reiney was at the funeral and later gave it to Dick Holmes to sell, offering to share part of it with him. Tom believes she did this in order to avoid having to share it with Reiney for whatever reason. It is true Dick didn't have much of it to leave to his son. Of course, over the years pieces of it have shown up in private collections—or so it is said.

Reiney eventually left Phoenix and Julia. Both of their lives ended in tragedy. Perhaps Julia was angry with the boy because he didn't seem to want to pay careful attention to the details the old man was trying desperately to give him. Or, maybe Julia believed she needed what was there to carry her through until she located the mine site.

Later, she would spend years trying to find Jacob's treasure. Eventually, frustration and poverty would reduce her to drafting and selling maps to newcomers with gold fever. As the saga grew in Julia's mind and she became more confused—the maps changed along with her story. She must have enjoyed her celebrity, but certainly she was to be pitied.

Sims Ely last saw Julia in 1917, the year of her death, in a shack fronting on the south side of the Southern Pacific tracks. Totally disillusioned, broke and befuddled, Julia wept when Sims Ely offered her a handout.

The newsman was later quoted, "Hers had been a sad lot indeed."

* * *

This seems an appropriate time to evaluate the facts thus far. Two local newspapers duly noted Jacob's death and the time and place of the burial. Brownie's father documents the John Phipps story. So far John is the first recorded victim of the curse. Had the cowboys been successful in releasing the miner from the cave-in, he would have had no choice but to reveal the mine's exact location. Unfortunately for Dick Holmes that rainy night, John told him a story of untold riches.

Greed ruined Dick Holmes' life and later, his son, Brownie's. The fact of the mine's existence seemed to incur wrath on all who knew of it.

That Julia and Reiney were victimized also becomes obvious as the story progresses.

Chapter 2

The Dutchman

A list of chronological research and documents authenticating the existence of Jacob Waltz is necessary to this book. To avoid slowing the pace of an otherwise fascinating story we will discuss them briefly.

Suffice to say, the reader is well aware at this point that Waltz did exist and departed this "veil of tears" on October 25, 1891.

All interest now centers on two questions: How did Waltz find the mine? and Where is it located?

The first question will be answered through interviews with Julia, Reiney and others. Somewhere in between the lines lies the real truth, but the story appears genuine, give or take a few trivial differences. To answer the second question will require a great oracle, a good psychic or perhaps, another 100 years of total dedication on the part of literally hundreds of men and yes, even a few women. And, after one has absorbed the contents of this book, examined the evidence and realized the tragedy incurred by all of those who found it, one can only speculate why anyone would continue to search for it.

During May of 1985, through the auspices of Dr. Bertol Koester, the Honorary German Consul for Arizona, we were privy to the Waltz Clan via records held in Wurttemberg, Germany, where Jacob was born. Doctor Koester's connections within the government opened the necessary doors and church records.

Oberschwandorf, Wurttemberg is a small village nestled on the edge of Germany's beautiful Black Forest. Today the town looks much the same as it did when it was a Barony belonging to King William of Wurttemberg.

Doctor Koester arranged for our meeting to be held in the city hall of the now divided town. The two mayors, Hugo Meroth and Walter Gutekunst, were present at that meeting. That interesting experience was further heightened by a peek into the ancient town records which listed the Waltz clan.

Much discussion has been given over the years to the inconsistent spelling of Jacob's last name. At least six different versions had surfaced and all were explained.

Within this book there are five documents which were signed by Jacob while he lived in the United States. These include his application for naturalization, citizenship papers, a barley receipt, a signature on a petition to the territorial governor asking for protection for prospectors against the Apaches, and a document on claim jumping filed by Jacob Waltz in March of 1872. Now to add further proof, in the town records of Wurttemberg, Germany his name is spelled Waltz.

According to Mayor Meroth, historian of Wurttemberg, all of the Waltz clan were weavers. They were otherwise uneducated and it was not uncommon for them to misspell the name as many of them could barely write. At that particular time the family was in desperate straits. Famine, unprecedented cold winters, poverty, sickness and death had their undivided attention. At least 15 of them emigrated to America in 1846. Jacob was one of them. He was 38 years old at the time of his arrival in New York.

We visited Jacob's home and found a distant relative still living there.

At first Jacob helped out in a cousin's tannery until wanderlust took him to the goldfields of Meadow Creek, North Carolina, and Georgia. That same year he was in Natchez, Mississippi, declaring his intentions to become a citizen.

Rumors of the California Gold Rush ran rampant across the young nation and caught up with the German immigrant. He must have made his way with many others for the next record we've uncovered shows Jacob Waltz becoming a naturalized citizen of the United States of America in Los Angeles, California, in July of 1861.

In Sims Ely's book we are told that Jacob and his partner, Jacob Weisner, were soldiers. Historically that would be the time of the Civil War. It also is believed that the pair fought for the South. One might speculate that having failed to acquire any gold from the fields in the southern states, he signed up in order to survive. In 1864, however, his name appeared on Arizona's territorial census, one year before the Civil War ended. Although one can only conjecture, it might be reasonable to assume he deserted the Army after realizing that the South was going down in defeat. Depending on his location at that time he might have decided to keep on going and try his luck at prospecting in the West.

According to claims filed at the time of the 1864 territorial census, Jacob was in the Walker mining district near Prescott. He filed claims on Turkey Creek. Obviously, he was prospecting California and Arizona territories.

Since he was born in 1808, Waltz was then 56 years old.

Later, as his name became a legend, stories of mining ventures rose out of that lore connecting him to the Vulture Mine near Wickenburg, Congress, Stanton and Rich Hill. All of those Arizona ventures were rich strikes. There is every reason to believe the Dutchman, at least, went to those mines or was in the general area, but his name does not appear on any of their ledgers.

No one would question the fact that the man was a loner, yet when he arrived in the Salt River Valley (where Phoenix was located) he became acquainted with Jacob and Andrew Starar. The pair were new arrivals from the "old country" and Waltz probably felt a tie. The year was 1867.

The Germans were working with Jack Swilling, one of Phoenix's early pioneers, on an irrigation system. Swilling made use of foreigners, especially the German immigrants, because of their willingness to work. The famous Dutchman's Ditch

Jacob Waltz's claim on Turkey Creek, 1864.

Jacob's signature as it appears on an application to Territorial Governor for protection from the Apaches.

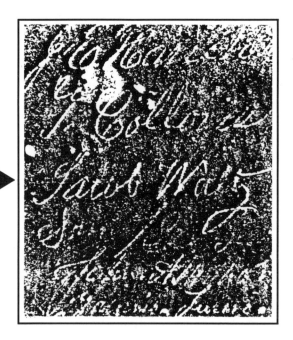

*Affadavit of Claim Jumping filed in Pinal County by
Jacob Waltz in 1872.*

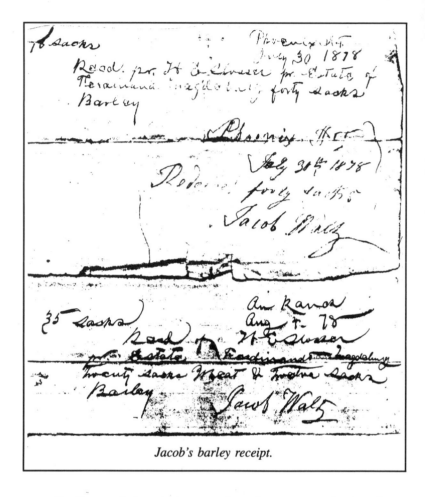

Jacob's barley receipt.

actually fostered the city's growth and was named after those whose toil and sweat built it.

In March of 1868 Waltz homesteaded 160 acres north of the Salt River. Apparently he had decided to become a farmer until wanderlust caught him again.

None of the records indicate that Jacob Weisner was with him at that time. An interview which appears in Chapter 7 with Tom Weedin, editor of the *Florence Blade* and onetime candidate for governor, may change the reader's mind. Still that fact cannot be proven.

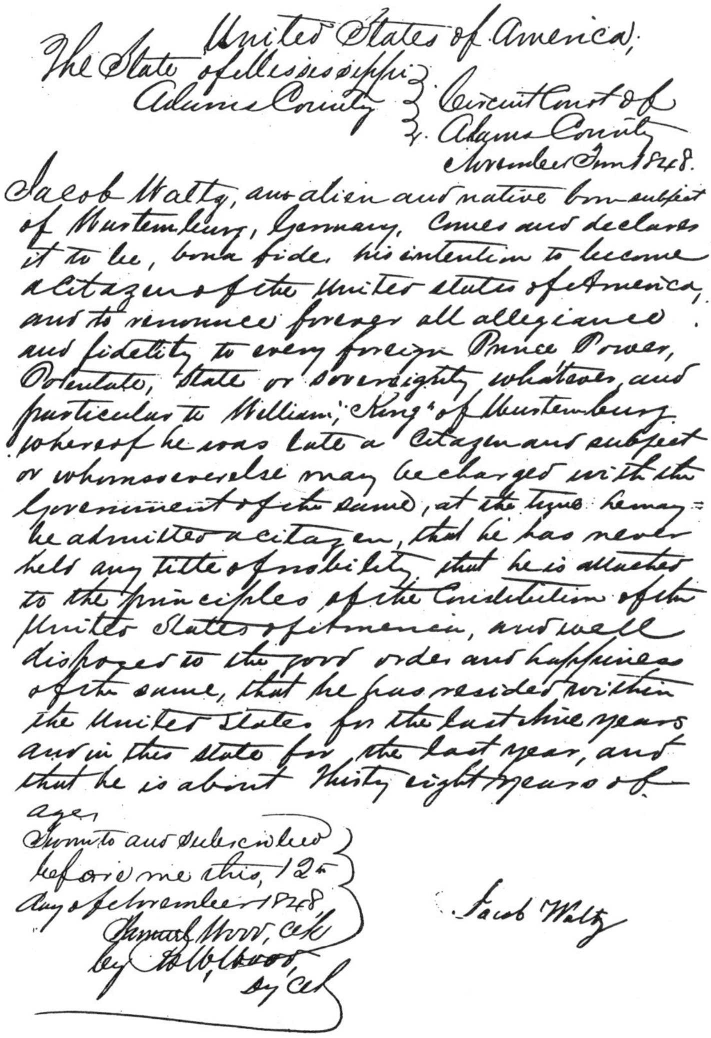

Jacob Waltz's petition for citizenship, 1848.

STATE OF CALIFORNIA.

IN THE 1st Dist COURT OF THE COUNTY OF LOS ANGELES. Cal.

In the matter of the application of

Jacob Waltz

to be admitted a Citizen of the United States.

Foreman an COUNTY OF LOS ANGELES, ss: *Jacob Waltz, Antan*
of said County, being duly sworn testifies and says: That he is well acquainted with the above
named *Jacob Waltz* and has been so acquainted with
him for five years, and that the said *Jacob Waltz* has
continually resided within the limits and under the jurisdiction of the United States of America
for five years, last past, and for one year, last past, within the State of California, and that,
during such time, he has behaved himself as a man of good moral character, attached to the
principles of the Constitution of the United States, and well disposed to the good order and
happiness of the same,

Anton Fredhmann

Subscribed and sworn to, in open Court, this
19 day of *July* —A. D. 1861,

John M Shore

Clerk.

STATE OF CALIFORNIA, } ss.   I, *Jacob Waltz* do
COUNTY OF LOS ANGELES
solemnly swear, that I will support the Constitution of the United States, and that I do,
absolutely and entirely, renounce and abjure, all allegiance and fidelity to all, and every, foreign
Prince, Potentate, State or Sovereignty, whatever; and particularly to
William King of Wurtemberg

Subscribed and sworn to, in open Court, this
19th day of *July* — A. D., 1861,   *Jacob Waltz*
before me,

Jacob's citizenship document, 1861.

FOUL MURDER.

A Mexican Killed by a Supposed Friend.

The Cause of the Base Crime Shrouded in Mystery.

ARIZONA *GAZETTE*
WEDNESDAY JUNE *18*, *1884*

About 10 o'clock this morning word was received that a Mexican by the name of Pedro Ortega had been murdered, at the house of Jacob Waltz, one mile southeast of this city, by a man named Selso Grajalva. The matter was turned over to Justice Richards, who, acting as a coroner, summoned a jury and repaired to the scene of the tragedy at 1 o'clock. The GAZETTE reporter was on hand. He found the body of Ortega lying about thirty feet from the house of Jacob Waltz, his legs and abdomen from the knees to the breast bone were perforated with "double B" shot, the femoral artery on the right side being severed and in itself producing death. There is a mystery about the entire affair. Ortego was shot and killed by a shotgun belonging to Jacob Waltz. That gentleman heard the Mexicans talking loudly, and then the report of a gun. He ran to the side of the house where the tragedy occured and saw the dying man. The assassin evidently ran around the building in an opposite direction, returned the gun to the room and place from whence it had been taken, and then sought flight. Waltz did not know, and so testified at the inquest, that his gun had been the instrument of the crime

until Deputy Sheriff Rogers appeared on the scene. The only direct testimony was that of Waltz. Two Mexicans swore that Ortega and Grajalva were the best of friends; that they saw them together this morning, and no hard feelings apparently existed. Both were laborers. Grajalva had secured a little job from Jacob Starrar to do some hoeing. Ortega, prior to this, had announced to his friends his intention of coming to town. Grajalva secured two hoes evidently expecting Ortega to assist him in his work. Right here we have the only possible motive for the crime. Ortega may have refused to assist Grajalva in the work, which so incensed the man as to bring about the murder. This is hardly a rational view, but as there were no grounds for jealousy, and as both men were entirely sober, we can conceive no other reason for the murder, which was not witnessed by human eyes. The flight of Grajalva is conclusive of his guilt.

The verdict of the jury was to the effect that Ortega had come to his death from wounds from a gun, supposed to have been discharged in the hands of Selso Grajalda. The murderer is still at large, although officers are in hot pursuit.

*This article appeared in the Arizona Weekly Gazette. Once again,
it reinforces the location of Jacob's farm outside of town.*

Tom Kollenborn believes Jacob must have found the mine sometime after 1872 but before 1878.

The Peralta story, as told by Jacob in this chapter, did not appear in print until after 1920. It is important for the reader to remember newsmen were in a heyday of romantic escapades. Life in the West was grist for their journalistic mill. So-called civilized Easterners, hungry for the tales coming out of the frontier, literally sopped up stories glamorizing the rugged life. Many a career was enhanced by news accounts of heroic settlers, dreaded Indian warriors, death and the thrill of treasure seeking. They are still considered the most famous 40 years in America's history.

Many fortunes were being made in Arizona. The cry of bonanza filtered out of burning sands, across the wheatfields of Kansas, into the lush Ohio Valley, through the timber of Virginia, to the country's Capitol. One can just imagine the gossip as it was carried onto the deck of a four-masted schooner bound for the sophisticated cities of Europe. America was, indeed, the land of opportunity.

Of all the theories surrounding the lost mine there were few facts to substantiate them. If Waltz had worked in the Vulture, his name would have appeared somewhere. Another theory was that he murdered two Mexicans to acquire his mine. Tom Kollenborn said in one of his journals, "This particular version has been fabricated to such a point, if any fact indeed did exist it would now be impossible to separate it from fiction."

There is a mining district just west of the Superstitions and east of the Goldfield Mountains, with the Apache trail transecting the area southwest to northeast. Many claim Waltz found the old Mexican arrastes at Mormon Flat and Government Wells. This search led him to either the rich Bulldog Mine or the Goldfield Mine.

The Bulldog had an 18-inch-wide, rich, gold-bearing vein. Waltz supposedly stated his gold came from a vein of quartz 18 inches thick. Was the gold in 18 inches of white quartz or pink? The Bulldog was found in white quartz. That claim was not filed until 1892, one year after the Dutchman's death. Maybe he didn't file on it to prevent a gold rush in that area.

Or, perhaps, Jacob Waltz found a cache. Some even believe he found a chimney of gold. Every theory has merit and an endless group of supporters to further perpetuate the legend. And, for those from other locales who find that hard to believe, this reporter has seen the groups who gather regularly just to view Tom Kollenborn's slide presentation of the canyons Jacob traversed. Every year there is a parade in Apache Junction to celebrate, and the now-famous Dons Club has its annual trek into Jacob's intriguing mountains. Hundreds of people come to Arizona annually just to search, and so the saga continues.

From 1873 to 1876 the prospector searched the area east of the Gold Field Mountains. He recovered gold from somewhere, the sale of which was reported by eyewitnesses in the Florence area.

After a long illness, during which it is presumed he thought he might die, the Dutchman deeded over his homestead to Andrew Starar. An agreement was signed and duly recorded that in return Starar would care for the old man for the rest of his life.

In this day and age of lawyers, accountants, wills and the IRS, one might find the matter an oddity but miners were a lonely lot. It was not uncommon for this kind of deal to be struck, particularly with foreigners who had neither wife nor child in America and were uncertain what relatives were left abroad. Remember, the Arizona territory was a rough place, life was cheap and greed high on man's list of sins.

Fortunately, Jacob recovered and was shortly seen heading for the mountains again. Many men followed him; they stated so publicly. Some of those stories are interesting reading and will surface in a later chapter. Suffice to say Jacob was tough. Most men believed he had murdered to get his mine and would do likewise to keep it. He had had run-ins with trackers on several occasions and told them, quote, "Follow me again and I'll kill you." No one doubted the man.

A prominent Mormon family gave the following statement of a story handed down from generation to generation of an eyewitness account overheard in an early Mesa store in 1884:

45

Yes, I recall the old man the day he came into our store for supplies. The skin of his face was parched dry from the desert sun and as hard as leather. His beard was almost snow white and somewhat stained by tobacco below his chin. His hands were coarse and calloused revealing many decades of hard work. He no longer stood erect for his age was now showing. His clothes were dusty and torn but were neatly in place.

The only reason I noticed him was he looked like my aging father. No one at first paid him any attention until he went to pay for his supplies. In his wrinkled hand was a small cowhide poke. He loosened the strings and poured onto the counter yellow gold in a matrix of white quartz. After gathering his supplies he left as quietly as he came.

Years later many witnesses recalled this encounter with the Dutchman. When questioned as to the direction he went most people were confused but it was the general consensus that he departed in an easterly direction toward the Superstition Mountains with his pack burro.

Six years later Jacob was dead. His secret died with him.

In 1886 Andrew Starar was evicted from the land on which he was living for non-payment of taxes. It was rumored he moved in with Julia to the shack where Jacob later died.

Jacob still owned his own land and was farming there. One might suppose that Jacob might have deeded a piece of his homestead over to his friend, but that was never proven.

Perhaps, when Jacob survived the first illness Starar tore up the original agreement for a small piece of land—again only Jacob and his friend knew the truth and they will never tell us now.

No researcher could discount Sims Ely's book or Jim Bark's handwritten notes. Both were men of good reputation whose systematic search for the truth was endless. They followed every clue, interviewed friends, acquaintances, locals, travelers and merchants who knew the man. Their personal search for the mine went on for years and, although they never found it, they left the world with the only account of what really happened. After my own efforts I have no reason to doubt them. Their words ring true and they often dealt with others of substance whose relatives were around to accost them. It seems unlikely that they would have had any reason to lie about the facts.

Ely, of course, eventually wrote a book admitting that their search, although futile, had been an avocation for more than half a lifetime.

This chapter, however, would never be complete without the conversation extracted from Julia regarding Jacob's location of the mine. It took place one afternoon in the sun outside the old man's adobe house.

"Now that I've told you this much," he said, "you have a right to know how I came upon the mine in the first place. It is a long story, and you must listen carefully.

"My partner's first name was Jacob, same as mine. His last name was Weisner. We were boyhood friends in Germany, our families lived near each other in St. Louis, and when the war broke out, we went to New Orleans and joined the Confederate Army together.

"We were so close it was almost the same as if we were brothers. When the war was over, we went by boat from New Orleans to Panama, and then to San Francisco. For a time we worked as clerks in the shipping office there. We made good wages because we were educated in German and English, but we thought we could make more money mining. So we tried it in California, and afterward we went to Mexico on a boat. We prospected aplenty in Mexico, but it got us nothing and we were plumb discouraged when we came to a little town in Sonora."

Helen and Reiney could never remember the name of the town but on his second trip to Mexico to check on Waltz's story, Jim Bark learned it was Arispa.

"There was a fiesta going on," Waltz said, "and a gambler was running a game dealing cards on a blanket, and nearly always the gambler won. My partner and I watched, and even though we weren't gamblers ourselves, it didn't take us long to realize the game was crooked as they came. And sure enough, a hand or two later, a man who had been losing heavily called the gambler a cheat. Quick as a flash, the gambler drew a knife and stabbed the man in the shoulder with a knife. Weisner was always the impulsive one and without a word he jerked his pistol from the holster and hit him senseless. I guess it made him pretty popular with the crowd because they just looked on quietly while we helped the man who'd been stabbed. We helped ourselves to the gambler's pile and gave the money to the injured man and then, we took him home. That man was Miguel Peralta. He had a nice place and many servants, but he was a lonely man all the same, a widower without children. So we stayed at his house until he got well. He found out that we were prospectors, and we fitted in with his own plans, because when he was up and about again he told us about his mine in Arizona."

Julia said at this point the old man shifted in the chair, fussed with a pipe and was momentarily silent, apparently coming to a crucial point in the story and wanting to choose the right words.

"Peralta said it was one of the richest mines in the world. It had been in his family for three generations—his grandfather, his father and himself. He said the mine was part of a church grant, which covered a large area. But in spite of the wealth that was theirs for the taking, the Peraltas had gone to the site only when badly in need of money. The Apaches had been bad, and after they had killed his father, Don Miguel was real afraid to take a long march in secret through Indian country. But now he was hard up and he wanted to take the chance if we would go along with him. Because we had been soldiers, he thought we'd be worth more to him than all of his peons. And if we'd go, we could have one-half of what was taken from the mine. Oh, it was a good proposition in most ways, but there were the Apaches to think about, and I wasn't sure. Weisner finally won me over, and we told Peralta we'd go with him. Poor Jacob, he was signing away his life without knowing it."

Julia saw emotion rising in the old man whose voice grew gruff as he paused to blow his nose. She reached over and rested a consoling hand on his arm.

Waltz resumed his story, his words were clipped, almost as if he'd lost interest.

It seems safe to assume that this was a traumatic moment for

Jacob; it must have been the first time he had ever recounted the story to anyone.

"Peralta made a good outfit," he went on. "Many animals, many peons, all armed. Peralta, Weisner and I had two horses, two rifles apiece, and pistols. We had waited for the summer rains in Arizona so there would be plenty of grass for our animals. We were two weeks on the road, and we had worked at the mine for several more. The peons did the work mostly. The ore was in a pit. It was wonderfully rich, and easy to take out of the rock. The Apaches never once came to our camp—at least, we didn't see any. On the way back we stopped at Tucson to sell our gold. Peralta kept his word and gave us half. It came to nearly thirty thousand dollars. Our share, that is."

Helena and Reiney's exclamations were quickly silenced as the German went on.

"Even then my partner had his chance," he said soberly. "We had plenty of money now to go into business for ourselves in San Francisco, and we should've done it. But Peralta wasn't willing for us to leave him just yet, and he was a mighty persuasive man. So we went on to Sonora with him.

"Back in his own place, Peralta began talking about his debts, and he made us a proposition. If we'd give him nearly all of our earnings, he said he'd let us have the mine for ourselves until we'd paid ourselves back, with a satisfactory profit besides. Of course, we'd made the trip once without a mishap. And, we'd seen the mine with our own eyes for what it was. After Don Miguel had explained all the ins and outs of it, we accepted. He gave us a paper making us temporary owners of the mine, and we turned over to him all our money except what we needed for a good outfit.

"To tell the truth, we weren't sorry at all to make that kind of trade with Peralta. Why, the ore in that mine was so rich you just wouldn't believe it. The nuggets of gold simply fell out when you crushed the rock with hammers.

"The mine was a round pit, shaped like a funnel with the large end up. Shelves had been made in the wall as the miners went deeper, and on each shelf stood upright timbers with notches in them for the miners to use in climbing out of the pit with

49

the sacks of ore on their backs. The pit was sloping to a point because the workers had shaped it that way. When Weisner and I were working the mine alone, one of us would stand guard with the rifle till the other came up with a sack of ore, then we'd separate it on canvas.

"Don Miguel's father had started a tunnel in the hillside, down below. It pointed straight toward where the ore would lie, deeper down. But Don Miguel himself didn't do any work on the tunnel, and Weisner and I weren't interested either. We knew we could take out enough gold for ourselves without bothering with that.

"Oh yes, it looked like a good trade alright. But it turned out to be the sorriest one we ever made. We had a piece of bad luck, in fact, the very first day we reached the mine."

Julia said to Sims, "At that moment Jacob stopped talking and it seemed to me and the boy that he never would resume. But there was something in his manner which forbad prodding," and so they waited, on the edge of their seats.

"We made the trip alright," Waltz finally said. "We'd got ourselves six good horses and a mule, and we had our rifles and pistols, tools and provisions and plenty of money. We rested a day on the Gila, in a Pima village, and bought some supplies before going on and put fresh shoes on our horses where they were needed.

"Just a few miles from the mine we found water and we stopped there to make camp. There was water nearer the mine at this time of year, we knew, but it was safer to have our camp some distance away. We planned, actually, to do just as Peralta had done. That is to say we would ride between the camp and the mine and leave the extra animals hobbled near the camp. Then we'd take each day's cleanup with us when we left the mine and store that gold in a cache near the camp—someplace where nobody could find it. So we got off our horses and hobbled them, and then carefully, on foot, we went toward the mine. As we got near the top of the ridge, we heard noises. Somebody was breaking rock over on the other side. Quietly we crept to the top and looked down. There were two men down there, and they were hammering rock. They were naked from the waist up, and their skins were brown, and with a kind of chill we decided that they were Apaches. 'Let's look around,' we whispered to each other, 'to see if there are any more.' We reconnoitered, but we saw no more Apaches, and at last we crawled back to the top of the ridge. We'd shoot those two Apaches, we decided, and bury them.

"Maybe a man's entitled to a few mistakes in his life, I don't know, but this was certainly one of ours. We could have gone back to camp and waited a day or two for 'em to clear out. Still we couldn't know just how long they'd stay, and we were impatient, I guess, to get the gold. Anyway, we took good aim and we shot them. But a horrible surprise awaited us when we ran down to the bodies. These weren't Apaches, we saw, but Mexicans, and on top of that we recognized them as two of Peralta's peons. Peralta had told us it wasn't uncommon for some of his people to poach at the mine, and sometimes they got killed by Apaches. Only we weren't Apaches, and we had killed two harmless, friendly men. We felt awful bad, both of us, looking down at those dead men, and I know I shed tears. So far as I knew, I'd never killed a man before, and though I'd seen many dead men in battles, I never felt easy about it. Now I'd killed one of those poor Mexicans. I tell you I've never gotten over it. Ever since that day I've felt guilty. And I know my partner felt bad about it, too, for he was a good man."

This obviously was the reason Waltz was forever-after labeled as a murderer. And, yes, he and Weisner had killed the men in cold blood. But, considering the life in the Superstitions against savages whose dedication appeared to be to kill all white men—the act was understandable. The conversation, if true, was taking place twenty years after the fact and he still evidenced tremendous remorse.

"Well, we buried the two Mexicans," Waltz said, "down the canyon, where there was dirt we could dig into, and then we went back to camp. We couldn't work any that day. And it didn't make us feel any better to know we hadn't been in danger from Apaches. But next day we bestirred ourselves and began working the mine. We kept it up until sundown, and after that we worked hard as we could, every day for many weeks. We took out much gold, and every night we took it away with us and placed it in a cache we'd made. We didn't take it easy the way Peralta's peons had done—I guess two men never worked harder. I'd say we placed twenty thousand dollars worth in the large cache—that's the gold we'll bring out in the spring—then we started on the two smaller caches. We'd put several thousand dollars worth in each of those when calamity hit us with all four feet.

"It was that infernal mule. You know how it is, mules won't leave horses, so we'd let the beast wander around without hobbles. This night I'm tellin' you about, the rogue mule wandered to the tree where we'd hung our sacks of flour, hams and the like. We'd thought that in the branches those provisions were out of reach of wild animals, to say nothing of a mule. Somehow the confounded critter managed to reach the flour sacks with his teeth. He wasn't content with one sack of course. Instead he pulled 'em all down, and all the flour spilled out. He ate some of it and walked in the rest.

"So there we were without flour, and there was nothing for us to do but to go to Adams Mill, on the Gila, for more. It seemed like a small chore for two men, and was decided that I'd go alone. I'd ride one of the horses and lead another, and I'd bring some other stuff besides the flour. Weisner would work around the mine while I was gone."

Waltz paused to look at young Petrasch, reflectively, and when he next spoke, he directed his words toward the boy. "Reiney," he said, 'you're too young to know, probably, and maybe it'll never happen to you anyway, but sometimes it does seem that you make one mistake—sow one seed—and then you reap a harvest of 'em. It was that way with us. Oh, it's easy enough to see now. Either Weisner should have waited in camp while I was gone or we should have gone away together. But there it was—I'd be away the better part of four days, and Weisner could accomplish a lot in that time, work that needed to be done. So I left him. And, I never saw him again.

"You can just see, Reiney, how one thing led to another. When I got to the Gila, I spent the night with the Pimas and next morning, when I was ready to start back, I noticed a shoe was loose on one of the horses. Should have examined the horses' feet that night, when I got in, but I was foolish and didn't. Then the next morning, when I saw the loose shoe, the Indian that did horse-shoeing wasn't there. He'd gone out hunting rabbits, and he didn't come back until late. He got the horse shod, finally, and I made up my mind to start back that night, make a dry camp, and in that way get back to the mine early the day afterwards. Maybe it was intended to work out the way it did. If it was, I'd been carrying an extra burden all these years. But, yes or no, Mr. Adams then discovered he was short of flour. He'd sold more than he expected that day, and there'd be no more grinding until the next morning. So there was a whole day lost. I didn't get back to camp until late the fifth day.

"One day—twenty-four hours or so—and it made all the difference. Because I took that fifth day, I caused the death of my partner, just as sure as shootin'. Leastways, I've always felt that way, I caused the death of Jacob Weisner, my best friend and I've never forgiven myself."

Ely said, "Warm-hearted, generous Helena would have protested but Waltz seemed not to hear her. It was as if his story, bottled up all these years, were now telling itself."

"It was still light enough for me to see, when I got back to camp," Waltz said. "It had all been destroyed, and there wasn't an animal in sight. The only sign of my partner was his shirt hanging on a bush. From what I know of Apaches, they had attacked him, alone as he was, and taken him away and tortured him. There was a Masonic pin on the shirt, and they would have left that behind, thinking it bad medicine. For awhile I just sat there stupefied amidst the poor remains of our camp, and then I roused myself. I hid one of my horses in the brush and hobbled him, and the other I rode in a lather to the mine, hoping against hope that Weisner might be there. The moon had come up, and I could see everything as plain as day—more than I wanted to. That camp was destroyed, too—everything gone but one frying pan, and the Apaches had driven a pick through it. There was no chance now that Weisner had escaped, and there was nothing to do but get out of those mountains fast. I went back for the other horse and then hurried to the caches. They

THE CURSE OF THE DUTCHMAN'S GOLD

hadn't been disturbed, and I took the gold out of one of the two small ones, covered the place over, and started away, leading one horse. Somehow I got out of the mountains without seeing or hearing Apaches. I guess they'd moved on by then. I did stop at the first water hole, but only long enough for the horses to drink, and I didn't really feel safe until I was far out on the desert and it was daylight and I could see a long way in all directions."

Jim Bark's notes jibed with Sims' story basically. But Jim had questioned Reiney over and over again trying to ferret out the truth. There were some discrepancies—small things which the boy probably had thought unimportant. Reiney said, "The frying pan had a bullet hole in it." Bark insisted no Indian ever wasted a bullet that way. Sims and Julia reported it was a pick. The pick was a tool used in mining the ore—one might imagine an Indian doing that as a symbol to the white man not to try mining there again. Remember Indians had no use for ore and it was gold which enticed the white-eyes into their sacred mountains. The Apaches were fierce adversaries who used torture on their victims. They were feared by whites, Mexicans and other Indians alike. And, yet, white men still persisted in the search, but after that time few Mexicans came north to mine.

Jim Bark also didn't believe the Apaches had left the shirt. Perhaps, Ely added the part about the Masonic pin to explain the item left in camp. Apaches always stripped their captors then later wore their clothing as a badge of victory, or perhaps as souvenirs.

Men have always done that in war. Americans were no different. Everyone of a certain age remembers seeing Japanese and Nazi flags, guns and articles of clothing exhibited all over the United States after World War II.

But, Jacob had made a good point—the Apaches were certainly superstitious.

There is one other factor in this point. Reiney was of German extraction from a poor family. He probably didn't know what a Masonic pin represented whereas Julia had grown up in the

United States working in shops where it is possible she had noticed such an item and even inquired about it.

The fact of the stripping of the victims would be a clue in two murders involving the soldiers which occurred later in this same story. Greedy white men soon learned the value of observing the savages' ways. Many murders were laid at the feet of the Red men in an attempt to cover up skullduggery by prospectors who thought they had found the elusive treasure at last. And, of course, there are other factors worth noting. Ely was a newsman given to romantic verbalizing—and, why not? However, he ended his book with a quote from Jim Bark which seemed to imply truth.

"In Jim's last years, he used to say, 'Hunting the Dutchman is not for old men.' Nor for old prospectors who sit on park benches in our western towns—and are still filled with hope, exaggeration, specimens and nicotine. They must step aside and let the younger generation hunt the Lost Dutchman, chew their own tobacco, tell their own lies and buy or steal their own specimens. . . . Someone, someday will fit the parts together more successfully than we have done. Good luck to him.' "

For a long time Tom Kollenborn did not believe Jacob Weisner existed. Obviously, the pair were more than inconspicuous in their travels. Germans, especially prospectors, were no novelty in the Territory during those times. Jacob Waltz probably didn't start getting notoriety until after Weisner's death and that was a fact tossed around by rumor and local gossip. More than likely real fame wasn't achieved until after his own death when the search for the mine began in earnest. Due to persistent dedication in his quest for truth, however, Tom found the amazing news clip which appears on the following page.

Because of the transient nature of the population in the Territory, it was customary for the United States Post Office to publish a dead letter list. In the *Phoenix Daily Herald* published September 22, 1896 (page 7, column 3) he found a list of

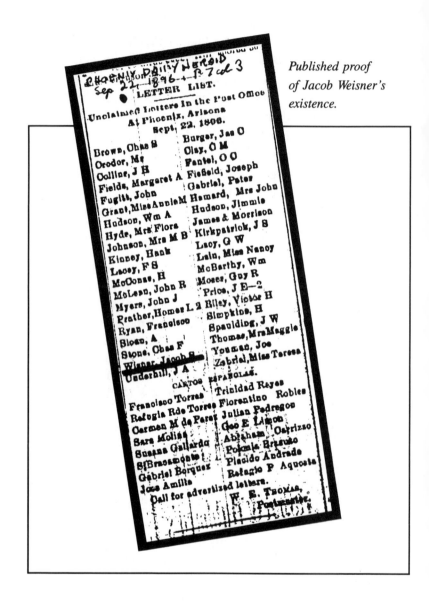

Published proof of Jacob Weisner's existence.

addressees for unclaimed letters which was separated into Anglos and Mexicans. Second from the bottom of the first column of Anglos is "Wisner, Jacob B." Proof the man did exist. Of course, the name is spelled slightly different, but that is understandable. The person who sent the letter probably misspelled it or, perhaps Ely did. It really is immaterial. There were no other persons ever recorded in the reams of documents Tom perused at mines, in federal offices, state archives and county recordings. He sincerely believes (since the middle initial is the same) it was Jacob's partner.

Chapter 3

Brownie's Words on Jacob's Last Moments

A s had been previously stated, two different stories exist
regarding Jacob's mine. The Petrasch and the Holmes
versions are worlds apart. One might think after reading the text
thus far that Brownie stands alone in his story; that is not so.
An entire group of collaborators supports Brownie's theory and,
believe it or not, two generations later that feud continues.

Brownie's notes were so voluminous that it wasn't practical
to reproduce all of them, but the most important things have been
included. It seems reasonable to expose this part of his story at
this time because Brownie's version differs from the others in
his appraisal of Jacob. Even if one wanted to believe the entire
unique tale, most people could not accept the fact that a dying
man, who could hardly breathe when Julia left to fetch the doctor, could have physically spent the time and energy it would
have taken to tell his story.

In all fairness to Brownie he must have loved his father, or
so it seems because he believed the story and defended it. One
might also accept the premise of his embitterment over two
lifetimes spent by the Holmes men searching in vain for something
they obviously believed was theirs.

Usually men mellow with age and by the time Tom Kollenborn interviewed Brownie, he was an old man. Brownie admitted

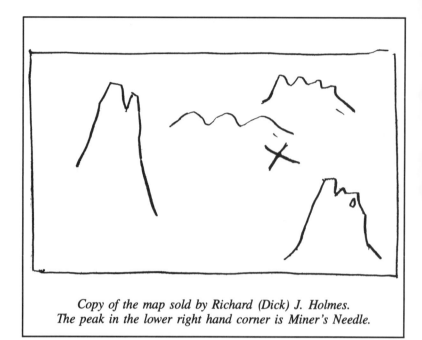

Copy of the map sold by Richard (Dick) J. Holmes.
The peak in the lower right hand corner is Miner's Needle.

to Tom, during an hour-long tape, that he regretted selling
the gold ore and the jewelry made from Jacob's ore, but he needed
the money to pay medical bills in his last days. Anyone would
sympathize with his plight.

Because of the Dutchman legend Brownie Holmes dedicated
his life to locating the treasure, and unfortunately, he had gold
that proved its existence. Brownie held a small treasure which
became an obsession.

You will find references to Brownie's character throughout this
text. It seems his destiny to wear a black hat in this mystery.

This lonely man lived in the great Superstition range until he
was too old to function there. His remembrances of that place
include fear and strange sounds and sights. The curse plagued
him, but like so many others of his ilk, he went to his grave believing in the mine.

The following notes are Brownie's story of Jacob's last
moments.

HELEN CORBIN

THE TRUE STORY
OF THE LOST DUTCHMAN OF THE SUPERSTITIONS
AS TOLD TO MY FATHER, DICK HOLMES,
BY JACOB WOLZ ON HIS DEATH BED.

The old man was very sick and frequently, during his conversation, was compelled to rest for a moment. But in spite of his weaked condition he related the following: "Dick, I know that you've wanted to locate this mine—you tried to follow me once, and I might have killed you. I'm glad that I didn't because I like you—and there is no one I'd rather see find it than you. Years ago I worked in the Vulture at Wickenburg...I made a little stake and wanted to take a trip to Picket Post (Picket Post is located near where Superior now is). After I got there I didn't want to stay so I started back to the Vulture by the way of Fort McDowell over the Military Trail. This trail as you know is used by the soldiers at McDowell. This was in 1877. I had three mules with me and a pretty fair camping outfit—that I had bought a few months before. First night out from Picket Post—I guess I was about fifteen miles from there—I made camp. Next morning about dawn—just as I was about to start fire, to make some coffee—three Apaches came running towards my camp. I knew the ornery devils were after me...We played hide-and-seek among the rocks for quite a spell—and I knew they'd get me sooner or later—so I slipped out of the arroyo and got away from them. They looked for me for a while—I guess—and then made off with my outfit. That's all they wanted anyway. Well, there I was afoot with no water and no breakfast. I had gotten off the trail considerably and was pretty much lost. I know general directions to the Fort but it was a long way off. I had to keep close watch for other Indians because that whole country was full of them and they were pretty damn mean too. I didn't go very far that first day because the country was rough and in some places I'd have to walk a half mile to get around a rough canyon. That night I found a cave in the side of a hill. It was full of bats and every once in awhile I heard a noise a lot like a rattler. But I would rather sleep with the bats and the rattlers too than take a chance on them damn Apaches. Early next morning I started out again. I had not had any grub since the Indians ran me out

61

of my camp and my feet were getting sore. I had just crossed a wash and got up the other side, when I saw human footprints. So I followed them. They looked like they were fairly fresh—and they pointed in the general direction of Fort McDowell." (Here the old man stopped and rested and felt of his side and emitted a suppressed groan as a sudden severe pain had pierced his congested lungs. After a short interval he continued.) "I had only followed the trail for about half a mile when I came upon a camp. I could tell by the size of the outfit there was more than one person belonging to it. There wasn't a soul about—but there was grub and water. It wasn't Indian grub either and after I tasted some of it I know it was white man's grub and I ate plenty. I didn't drink much water though just took a sip now and then till I quenched my thirst. It was just getting about sundown when I woke up—I had fallen asleep. I heard some voices and I jumped up and grabbed my rifle. Pretty soon three Mexicans came into camp. They looked friendly enough but they acted surprised to find me there. One of them who spoke fairly good English asked me what I was doing there—and I told them about the affair with the Apaches. They all laughed and said I could stay there with them until they were ready to go to Fort McDowell—which would be in a few days. They said I could go with them if I wanted to stay until they were ready or if I wanted to go ahead they'd fix me some grub. I was about in the notion of taking the grub and going on my way when I saw one of them unload a sack of ore from a burro. I asked them if they would let me see the ore. They were simple Mexicans and not at all suspicious so they let me take a look. Dick, that sack was full of gold ore. I asked them where the mine was located and they said I could go with them the next morning. I was still dead-tired when I went to bed but I couldn't sleep a wink thinking of that gold. *Next morning I went with them to the place about a quarter of a mile up the canyon from the camp.* They showed me the shaft and asked if I'd like to go down and take a look. The hole was only about four feet across and about twelve feet deep. I walked down the ladder and then I got to the bottom." (Here the old man paused again; it seemed to father that he was reliving the scenes of that exciting day; his feeble old hands shook as he

62

continued.) "There was the gold, Dick, wire gold in the rocks as large as peas. Several pounds of ore was lying on the bottom. On the bottom of the shaft I could see where they had been following the vein for just a few feet. It was about this thick." (Here he indicated the approximate thickness of the vein of rich ore with his hands—he held them about two feet apart.) "As the Mexicans worked, they talked freely. They told me they had only been working the mine a few months and that it had been originally operated by one Pedro Peralta, a Spanish Don. He had left Spain many years ago and had taken up residence near Mexico City. This Don Peralta made only three trips from Mexico to the mine; his party would consist of peon laborers, soldiers as escorts, their women and children and many animals, including cattle and sheep." (Here father interrupted the old man by admonishing him that he should rest for a moment. He wasn't particularly interested in the activities of the Peraltas and he realized the old man was sinking fast. What he wanted was the secret of the mine before it was too late. The old man waved aside his protestation and continued with his story.) "On these trips every precaution was taken to insure protection from the Apaches, who were always hostile towards the Mexicans, resenting their coming for gold and always attempting to raid the party to capture the animals and whatever else they could get. As means of protection, the Mexicans would herd their stock by day and place them in corrals at night under heavy guard. About 1858, after a winter of successful mining, the Peralta party broke camp and started his party on the long trip to Mexico. They were attacked by a large band of Apaches who were not as well equipped as the Mexicans—yet their number was greater and the Peralta party was handicapped because they had to defend their stock and women and children. Peralta tried to fight his way into the open country where he would be in a better position to defend the party. The Apaches guessed he would do this and were prepared for it. They tried to make their way to the west and then go over the slope of the mountain but they were completely surrounded by the Indians. All were massacred except one twelve-year-old boy who managed to make his escape during the battle. The lad found his way to a little Mexican settlement on the Gila River. The village people helped the boy make his way back to his people in Mexico. The lad never forgot the rich mine and in 1877 he returned with his two cousins and began working the property. The Mexican identified himself as the twelve-year-old boy and the other two Mexicans were the Cousins who had come to help with the mine. They explained to me that the early Spaniards put rocks in the forks of trees leading from the desert to the mines. Some of these rocks are so embedded now that they can only be removed by chopping them out. They took me into their confidence as though I was one of them. Their simple stories and absolute frankness—together with their extreme generosity impressed me not in the least. I had the gold lust in my blood, Dick—I made up my mind to get sole possession of that mine, at any cost. In a few days I saw my chance— they both had their backs to me. I grabbed my gun and shot them both. I had watched them closely and when one of them left and went to put some tools away as they were getting ready to break camp and go to Fort McDowell and had left the two alone with me. I saw my chance and took it. I covered the bodies and waited for the third man to return to camp. I didn't have to wait long. It seemed only a few moments until he came down the wash. I waited until he was fairly close to me before I shot him. (A pause and a noise coming from his throat that sounded very much like a whimper, the old man was extremely nervous now.) I buried their bodies close to their camp then took their outfit and went on to Fort McDowell. I stayed there two days, then came to Phoenix. I made another trip to the mine sometime later. I worked it for several weeks and took out several thousand dollars worth of gold. Before I made plans for my next trip I wrote to my sister in Germany and asked her to send her son over to help me. I sent her several thousand dollars and told her there was a lot more to be had. Soon afterwards the nephew arrived in Phoenix. I took him out to the mine. He hadn't been there long until he insisted on me recording the property and taking out all the gold at one time, rather than make secret trips every year. *I was not a citizen of the United States nor had I declared my intentions to become one*—so for that reason I couldn't locate and record the mine. That is according to law as if I had been a citizen. I was afraid there might be other Mexicans that knew of the mine and that they would come to investigate. I knew from the start that there would be trouble between my nephew and me because he was very quarrelsome and pretty much the type to tell other people what to do. It got so bad that we were quarreling all the time and two or three times I thought he would strike me. Somehow I got to hating him as if he was a bitter enemy instead of a nephew. We left the mine one morning and started for Phoenix, by the way of Fort McDowell. That night we camped at Agua Escondido. We had a terrible argument that night, the worst we'd had before. The next morning when we got up he said, 'I'm going to record the mine myself, whether you want to or not.' The dying old man looked up at father when he got to this point of the narrative—tears were gathering in his fast-dimming eyes and he said feebly, "I shot him in the forehead between the eyes—I then took a piece of chain and, putting it around his neck, dragged him under a shelving rock and where the dirt was soft I dug—a grave—and buried him." (The old man was softly crying now—it was evident that the slaying of his nephew unnerved him far more than the other murders he had committed.) "I returned to Phoenix and when the people asked me where my nephew was, I told them he'd gone back to Germany. I took care of my sister, though, Dick—I guess I sent her over two hundred thousand dollars all together. When you locate the mine I want you to give a portion of it to her. Will you? (Father nodded his head.) After the confession of this, his fourth murder, the old man remained silent for several minutes—with his eyes closed—after which he rallied and indicated that there were more killings of which he must confess before he would give directions to the mine.)

Author's note: Permit me to digress from this story for a moment to mention facts which should precede Waltz's further confession. Fort McDowell was one of the main United States Cavalry posts in the Southwest. It was located near the Verde River about 35 or so miles northeast of Phoenix. There were several other posts in the Territory at that time. One of them was at Picket Post and another at San Carlos. Part of the duties of the soldiers was to escort pack trains through the mountains as well as carry mail between the various posts. The mail carriers on one route consisted of two men, who made the trip from Fort McDowell to Picket Post once a week. After a series of trips back and forth, the two soldiers began to appear at the Silver King with a considerable quantity of gold in their possession. They boasted of having found a place where there was plenty more. There came a time when they did not arrive at their whereabouts and their bodies were found a few days later within a mile east of Weaver's Needle in the Superstitions. Circumstances surrounding their condition indicated that they had been murdered and horribly mutilated by the Apaches.)

"I had been gone from the mine for several months, Dick," continued the old German, "and on the next trip took with me some lumber to build a rocker as I was wasting some of the finer gold. I had to abandon some of this lumber in a rough brushy canyon and on returning to the mine I found it had been disturbed. That gold had done something to me—somehow I felt I was the sole owner of all the Superstition country. It made me mad to see anyone going in the direction of this mountain. I made up my mind to hide for two days, and then two soldiers came up to the mine and began working it. They only worked for a few hours and then got on their horses and rode away. I followed them and killed them both. I made it look like Indians had done it. After I killed the two soldiers, I went back to the mine and took out some more ore, then back to Phoenix. When I returned the next winter I saw where someone else had been there. I knew then that I was going to have to do something if I intended to keep the mine. So I started concealing it so no one could find it. I enlarged the shaft two and one half feet all around and left a ledge about six feet below the surface. I then went up the mountain and sawed timbers the right length to fit the ledge. I worked all winter sawing, dragging, and placing those timbers. They're in the shaft now—criss-crossing to a depth of six feet. I left about two feet near the top so I could fill in with dirt and rocks. *No one will ever find it unless he finds the rock house down in a brushy canyon.* It's almost impossible to get there unless you know how. But when you get there and follow my simple directions, you can go straight to the mine. The hideout is well-covered, with a natural growth of brush and trees and is impossible to see until you are almost upon it. Well, Dick, I hid some of my belongings in the hideout and took what gold I had dug up and started out to Phoenix. About three miles from camp I met a prospector with two burros loaded with camping equipment." (Here the old man hesitated again and maintained his customary silence—his eyes closed.) "And I shot him without giving him a chance to explain where he was going or what his business was in the mountains. I drove his burros quite some distance from where I killed him. I unloaded the equipment and set fire to it, then drove the burros away." (Wolz thought in disposing the aged prospector he had eliminated the last man who knew of the mine's location or existence. He did not realize that at the time there was a man at that moment at the Silver King whose name was Deering, and who was gathering supplies to make a return trip to his mine.) "That prospector's death made seven men that I've killed, Dick—seven human lives over gold—and look at me now. My last trips were made by the way of the Salt River. Traveling up to Monroy's Ranch and taking the old Government Trail which crosses the river at that point and then following it into the Superstitions. I worked the mine for two weeks this winter before the rains set in. It was very cold and somehow the weather seemed to affect me more. One morning I had a chill. I knew there was something wrong and somehow I couldn't help but believe that I was on my last trip to the mine. I hid most of the gold I had gotten out and brought the rest with me. There's not much there, but after I am gone you can have it—it's in a box under my bed. Take it—I know there is enough to grubstake you for awhile anyway, Dick. Dick," the old man gasped, "I must tell you," he breathed laboriously and there appeared a peculiar pallor on his cheeks, as if his life's blood was quickly drawn away from his body. *"Go to First Water,"* he whispered, *"then to Second Water—then take the old Government Trail to San Carlos—where the trail turns south—you will see—over the point of the ridge—a rock—standing in the brush—*

it looks like a man. When I first saw it—I thought it was—a man—so one day I rode over to it—and with my pick—carved the eyes, the nose—and mouth on it, then I said—You look like a man so I'll make you a man. *This is where I always leave the trail.*" (His strength failed him and once again he lay with closed eyes.) Father thought he was dead. The peculiar pallor of his face seemed to become more noticeable and then he rallied with renewed strength and continued. "*Go to the left of the trail, follow up the long ridge and you will come to a saddle. In this saddle is a round Indian ruin of rocks. Go through this saddle and on up a low ridge and when you get on the highest point of the ridge you can look north and the Four Peaks are lined up to look like one peak. In the other direction you will see a high needle (pointed rock). In the canyon under you is my hidden camp. You can't get down there because it is too steep, but go to the mouth of the canyon and then back. You can find the rock house with very little difficulty. You won't be able to see it until you are right upon it. After finding the camp then come back out of the canyon.*" (Here he gave a direction to the mine.) "*You will never be able to find the mine until you first find the rock house as the shaft is completely hidden.* A prospector will never be able to find it because there is no ledge in view. In the mine you will find about $75,000 dollars in gold already dug out. *Be careful, Dick, in opening the shaft as I have set a trap that will instanty kill any person who accidentally finds the mine.*" Here father interrupted with: "Wolz, did you dig all the gold out or is there some left?" "There is enough gold to make twenty men millionaires," Wolz replied. And, holding his hands about two feet apart, continued: "*The ore is this wide and runs the mountain side about four hundred feet where it crops out in the bottom of a wash. I dug this cropping away and erased all signs of my digging. . . .*" (Here the old man stopped and rested for a while, and suddenly appeared to becoming weak again.) When he returned to his narrative he talked in a whisper. And the whispers became more faint as he went on. At times he would gasp for breath and clutch his breast faintly or weakly. "*Follow my directions and you will have no difficulty in finding the mine. First find the rock with the face on it—then the rock house—*

you—have—to do that. Don't forget to take the candle—the box of ore—under my bed. When you find the mine—send my sister—some money." He closed his eyes, taking a deep breath as if to continue the conversation. There was a slight stiffening of the giant frame, then a gurgling sound emanated from somewhere in his throat—and Jacob Wolz—sole owner of the fabulous gold mine of the Superstitions, was dead.

Father and Roberts remained at the bedside until the doctor arrived with the much excited housekeeper. It was fortunate, so far as listening to the story of the mine was concerned, that the colored woman had some difficulty in locating the physician. However unfortunate it might have been for poor Mr. Wolz, it is doubtful that anything could have been done anyway to save his life. The doctor gave the corpse a hasty examination and returned to the bedside of a woman who was soon to present the town of Phoenix with a new citizen to replace one who was no more. Father turned from his rather long and thoughtful observance of the corpse of Jacob Wolz to speak to the colored woman, but she had vanished. He then reached under the bed and brought out the candle box of ore—which the Dutchman said he could have. He and Roberts carried the box home, and ground the contents by hand, laying aside some of the specimens of quartz for future study. The gold content of the rich high grade ore was approximately forty-eight hundred dollars, which was a godsend to father at that time as he had left the Government Service as a packer to be near Mother, who was soon to bring another citizen of Phoenix into the world, no less than George Brownie Holmes. Father was at that time running short of funds as a result of unemployment. *I have in my possession at the present time a beautiful pair of cuff links, each of which contains an elaborate setting of polished quartz taken from the Lost Dutchman Gold Mine. In addition, I also have a slabbed match box made by a San Francisco jeweler, a tie pin and a priceless ring, together with a number of pieces of quartz.* Wolz was buried amid very simple ceremonies in the cemetery on West Madison Street in the City of Phoenix. This cemetery is today still in existence, but in a very sad state of repair. Within its boundaries have been buried some of the fore most pioneers of Arizona.

But it stands today unkept and unsightly instead of being a beautiful shrine, perpetually maintained with flowers and shrubbery as a token of reverence and appreciation for those who have helped make Arizona what it is today, and whose bodies are now reposing under unattractive soil, forgotten. In this same cemetery very close to Wolz's grave are buried my grandmother and grandfather; also an aunt and an uncle are buried there. Roberts and my father made a pact that neither of them would divulge what Wolz had told them and that they would share the mine if either found it. Roberts did not live as long, as he was the victim of silicosis and, when he passed away, father alone knew the story of the Lost Dutchman Mine. News of Wolz's death and of the fabulously rich mine he worked spread rapidly. The title of Lost Dutchman was given to the lost mine. Immediately its fame spread rapidly, far and wide. Various stories, some of them preposterous, began to circulate as to its origin and its location. Maps of various descriptions appeared frequently in hands of people who never had been in the Superstitions. Some of them were so impossible that even the most of tender-feet scoffed at them, yet they disclose the fact that some person or persons had already began to cash in on the mystery of the lost mine. Many people, thinking that the Negress housekeeper of the departed Dutchman was in full possession of his secret, treated her with special respect. This unexpected and unusual attention pleased the woman not a little and she began to manufacture all kinds of stories about the Lost Dutchman and its whereabouts. Her exaggerated stories were responsible for many futile expeditions being taken or undertaken. On many occasions she would go so far as to accompany a party on a search, for a consideration, and always on arriving near the range, become confused and then feigning illness, insist on being returned immediately to Phoenix. At last, when all her stories were proven without foundation, she admitted that my father was the sole possessor of the secret of the Lost Dutchman of the Superstitions. These statements, of course, turned the attention of the treasure hunters upon him before he had an opportunity to make his first trip into the mountains.

In this chapter Holmes quotes Jacob: "I was not a citizen

of the United States nor had I declared my intentions of becoming one—so for that reason I couldn't locate and record the mine."

As shown by the copy of Jacob's naturalization papers he became a recorded citizen of the United States in Los Angeles, California, in 1861. This conversation is supposed to have taken place in 1891.

Two important notes must be added at this point. Tom Kollenborn never was able to uncover any record of Jacob's having sent large sums of money back to his sister in Germany. In 1985 when this researcher questioned the two mayors of the now divided town of Wurttemberg, they both stated through my interpreter, Dr. Koester, that it would have been impossible for that much money to have entered the town undetected. Throughout all the years of discussion about Jacob Waltz no one ever mentioned that fact.

Holmes also discussed Jacob's murder of two soldiers who happened upon his mine. The story of the soldiers appears in Chapter 8 as revealed in the Bark notes and in Sims Ely's book. They are corroborated by Colonel Doran who knew both soldiers and was involved in the search for their bodies.

The entire matter has a direct bearing on other people who appear within the book. Gossip caused many theories to be accepted, but there seems to be more fact in the other accounts which cannot be disputed.

Chapter 4

Julia, Reiney
and the Man Called Jacob

R hinehart Petrasch's mother died in Denver when he was a baby. Julia offered to take him with the apparent approval of his immigrant father and brother, both miners. If he was ever formally adopted there is no record of it, but more than likely the agreement was verbal.

Julia called him Reiney. He was 16 when they arrived in Phoenix. Being of German descent, he spoke the language fluently thereby creating a natural bond with Jacob Waltz.

Sims Ely was quoted in his book as saying when the Dutchman first revealed the ore in the cans in Julia's living room/kitchen "Reiney, drawn irresistibly toward the ore, hovered over the table."

One can only imagine how intrigued a young man would be at such a moment, but being young he failed to comprehend the gravity of the situation or what Jacob's age actually meant to him or Julia.

Shortly after the old man's death, Julia sold the store. Confident of finding the mine, she spent money lavishly. After hiring a team and a light wagon, she and Reiney drove to First Water on the north side of the Superstition cliffs. They packed in from there. Waltz's instructions had been, *"You go over the mountain from the cow house and then down to a big spring."*

The cow house was reference to the Caveness dairy farm.

Neither one of them knew anything about the area. Their plan

73

Matt Cavaness' freight team at Gila Bend Stage Station in the 1880s.

was doomed from the start.

In Jim Bark's notes I found the following: "Reiney told me the first time he and Helena went over the mountain she got lost and as it was sundown, she became frantic. She got up on a large rock and stopped all night. She carried a small, 32 revolver and a lot of cartridges."

Jacob had certainly warned her enough times to the danger of being followed. She knew people would kill them just for information regarding its location. And, even though Julia didn't know where it was, the gossip in the cow town must have convinced everyone that she did. While she sat terrified on that rock pulling the trigger repeatedly against what she believed were rattlers, articles were being printed in local newspapers stating that she and the boy had rented a team and were headed for the hills. There was a later one published offering the information that she had returned and was unsuccessful.

When Julia had exhausted her efforts she wrote to Reiney's father and brother in Colorado. The pair were experienced miners

Julia and others search for Jacob's mine.

and the lady was desperate. At her urging they came. After the foursome had put in a futile year searching, Reiney quit in a fit of disgust.

Ely explained, "Julia and Reiney were very simple people able to absorb quickly and repeat almost verbatim conversations held with people they knew but, probably not able to retain details of something they really didn't understand."

The newsman sincerely believed that was the reason they were never able to find the mine. They just hadn't paid attention to the old German's exact description.

Of course, it was three years after the Dutchman's death when Sims Ely arrived in Phoenix. He was quoted: "Reiney had left the Phoenix area for good a year before I arrived." But, before he left Petrasch told all he knew about Waltz and the gold mine to Jim Bark at the latter's ranch. "The young man did this for two reasons," Sims said, "one, he was aware that Jim had known and respected Jacob Waltz and, two, he reached an understanding with Jim that the latter would do the right thing by Reiney,

Reiney Petrasch

Herman Petrasch, 1954

if he found the mine.

"Jim cross-examined the boy many times," Sims said. "And, also questioned Julia many times. We both agreed the results of both Jim's and my interviews all jibed . . . an important substantiation of the evidence."

Reiney Petrasch, the boy who was almost a son to the most famous prospector in the Golden West, put a shotgun to his head in 1953—another victim of the curse.

It seems critical to add the following information to this chapter.

Herman Petrasch, Reiney's older brother, became obsessed with the search. He moved into the Superstitions, eventually built a shack and with what his brother had told him, continued to search for the rest of his life. (His photograph appears with Reiney's in this chapter.) The brothers continually argued over the lost mine, so much so that a notorious feud developed between them. Their final argument was reputedly over the fact that Reiney had not paid attention to the old man's instructions and when questioned altered the facts. Reiney left the camp and the pair never spoke again.

Asylum where Reiney's father died and was buried.
Photo taken about 1900.

George Petrasch, a younger brother, died in Phoenix, Arizona, of dysentery on June 11, 1885. He is buried in the old city cemetery alongside Jacob Waltz. Gottfriet Petrasch, the father of the Petrasch brothers, must have married again after Julia took Reiney to Phoenix. Gottfriet was committed to the Arizona State Mental Hospital on December 1, 1913 and died there of bronchial pneumonia on May 22, 1914. He was buried in the hospital cemetery.

This time an entire family had been ruined.

Julia's story is equally interesting.

The Thomas family arrived in the summer of 1888 from Denver. Charley, Julia's husband, disappeared shortly after their arrival and was never heard from again. There was gossip that he ran off with another woman. He did, however, help her start the bakery. And, since the lady was a trained baker whose fresh bread rapidly became a local favorite, she was not going to be left destitute—at least, not yet.

Also, Julia had a foster son, Rhinehart (Reiney) Petrasch, then about 16.

Corner of Central and Washington Streets, Phoenix, AZ, 1884. Julia's store is in this group. No photo of Julia has ever been found.

Sims Ely wrote in his book, *The Lost Dutchman*, "I first questioned her [Julia] in 1896 and thereafter throughout the years."

Ely claimed the boy was adopted and perhaps Julia said as much, but one can only guess that no formal adoption ever took place. Life in the West in those days was informal and uncomplicated.

Julia was a mulatto woman reportedly from Louisiana while the boy was a German-Caucasian. They were, however, very compatible and enterprising.

Their bakery lease was on a frame building fronting on Washington Street to the north, one block east of the intersection of Washington and Central Avenue. The business was in the hub of the town at that time. Today that location is just east of Phoenix's County Court Building and Complex.

In due time the pair partitioned the store. On one side was an ice cream parlor which also served soft drinks and bread and butter; on the other they sold Julia's homemade treats.

The baked goods were prepared, in part at least, with fresh

eggs brought to her on a burro by an old man named Jacob Waltz who lived about a mile away in an adobe house near the river. Jacob looked forward to the trek. From all reports the lady was very kind. After each delivery there was a pleasant visit with the woman and the boy and the promise of a good home-cooked meal and hot bread. And, as the friendship cemented, even a haircut when one was needed.

Conjecture and Ely's interviews lead us to believe the old man was surprised when one afternoon he arrived to find Julia sitting at her bread table in tears. She was hovering over a pile of unpaid bills, especially the large one for a new soda fountain.

In those days Mexican peons would pay their last dollar for a soft drink or a watermelon, and their young ones loved ice cream. Unfortunately, they were usually broke. Julia, it seems, had extended credit to the tune of $600. According to Julia, Waltz took a look at her carefully compiled ledger and shook his white mane.

He had every reason to be grateful to the woman. And, since he didn't drink hard liquor, probably considered the visits as the high point of his social life. There was also the comfort of Reiney's fluency in German. They were often overheard talking in their native tongue.

Julia obviously thought Jacob to be a poor farmer and nothing else. Therefore, one can only imagine her surprise when he offered to help. She told Sims he said, "Send Reiney to me tonight, after you close up. You know I don't see well at night, and I want him to walk beside me and the burro."

Reiney told Jim Bark later, when he met the old man that night Jacob had a sack. And when Waltz mounted the burro Reiney heard the clink of metal against metal.

At the Thomas home Waltz ordered them to lock the doors and draw the shades. He then opened the sack and withdrew a number of tin cans covered with cloth which he immediately removed. The contents glowed in the lamplight.

Jacob said calmly, "I have $1,400 to $1,500 worth of gold in these cans. Tomorrow we'll ship it to a smelter in San Francisco through the express office. I've shipped gold from Casa Grande in the past; I'm familiar with the procedure. When the money comes back, I'll lend most of it to you, Helena."

He then swore them to secrecy, counseled her against bad business practices and told them he'd be back later to seal their bargain.

Later, in December of 1890, Waltz invited Julia and Reiney to his home beside the river for dinner. After the meal the party retired to wooden chairs outside to enjoy the pleasant afternoon sunshine. Jacob seemed withdrawn, fiddling with his pipe and saying little. Suddenly, as if a decision had been made, he said, "I want the two of you to know about that gold I've shipped. There's a great deal more where that came from—a great deal more. It's in a cache that we made, my partner and I."

The old man went on, Julia told Sims. "The gold came out of the mine, of course. It was taken out by the two of us and stored nearby. I have the right to work that mine, but I gave that up after my partner was killed. He was killed by Apaches twenty years ago, and I never wanted to work in the mine again. Anyhow, I'm getting too old for that kind of thing now."

Julia said Waltz became silent and the look of melancholy returned to his face.

(It is important to note at this point that all of the people who actually knew Waltz stated without exception that they recalled an innate sadness which he seldom overcame.)

Jacob went on, "Of course, Julia, you and Reiney couldn't do anything with a mine. You'd have to know about mining for that, and you'd need cash capital. Besides, the mine is in awful rough country, away from water—so rough that you can be right at the mine without seeing it. I wouldn't even try to tell you where the mine is if it wasn't for the cache. But you can't find one without the other. And the cache is different. All you need to do is bring the gold away, and we'll do that when spring comes. I'll give you half of that gold, Helena, and I'll keep the other half myself."

After that speech he became stern preparing for the admonition which followed. "You must both keep absolutely silent about this whole thing, all winter long, or we can't go. It's not so easy as you think. There are people who would follow us and kill us if they knew what we were after. I've kept the location of the mine a secret because I learned long ago if I don't keep my own secrets, I can't expect others to keep them for me."

"At this point," Julia confided to Sims, "the old man reconsidered and said, ' "On second thought, I don't think I'll tell you where it is—I'll just take you to it when it's warm enough to camp out.' " He further stated if they were wise they would guard the secret as he had. "All Mexican rights to the mine will die with me, and when I'm gone, you can sell the information about its location."

Jacob's eyes drifted toward the distant peaks, at least a day's ride away. In the waning light the Superstitions appeared a purple enigma. When at last the gaze drifted back he told them he had made three caches and that he already retrieved two of them on two separate occasions.

Julia and her foster son grew intense hearing him say the largest one was still there and the boy was immediately curious as to why he had never gone back.

Old Jacob was taking his sweet time telling the story. "I lived with the Pimas for many years after my partner was killed."

It was an accepted fact that the Pimas feared the Apaches. And, after guessing what the savages had done to his partner, Jacob Weisner, Waltz was afraid to go into the Superstitions alone.

Actually, Waltz's opinion stemmed from the fact of finding the camp in disarray, the animals missing and only his partner's shirt clinging naked to a shovel handle. The site bore the indelible mark of the Apaches, And the fate of the man he called friend was unknown, but if the Apaches had taken him he had died by torture.

Apparently, he still chastised himself even 20 years later for having stayed at the mill an extra day while picking up supplies.

Jacob went on. "After leaving the Pimas and traveling a bit, I returned to Arizona. Eventually, I settled in Phoenix and when the weather was right, I decided to go back to the mine." He elaborated on the preparation and the route he took and how he knew he was being followed. Pausing and hiding in the rocks, he finally spotted his tracker; then, out of caution, he backtracked and returned to his adobe home on the river.

The man who was following him had been in the Pima settlement twice. Jacob figured the Indians must have told him he had gold and had been mining in the Superstitions. Suddenly, Jacob's voice grew cautious as he said, "And, when we go there in the spring, we'll leave in the night."

As time went on Jacob became a steady visitor in Julia's home. He seemed to take comfort in the pair and treated the boy as a son. Little by little they heard the amazing story of the prospector's life after Weisner had been killed.

Describing his return to the mine the old man recounted how eerie the Superstitions appeared. The camp had been totally destroyed and the savages had stolen all of their equipment except for a frying pan—the Indians had driven a pick through that.

All Jacob wanted at that moment was to get out of the mountains with his scalp. He recovered a small cache as quickly as possible and hurried away in the night. A brief stop at a watering hole was his only pause and that had to be done to save the horses. He never saw an Indian but was constantly on guard with a shotgun. Jacob talked about spending that night at Adam's Mill and the next in Tucson. Finally, feeling much more secure he camped to give the horses a good rest before starting out for Sonora, Mexico. Actually, his destination was the Peralta Ranch. Jacob felt the need to tell a friend what had happened. After all, Peralta was the first man to tell him about the mine. He knew Weisner and would share the old man's grief, but upon arrival at the Mexican's ranch, he learned the man was away on a trip to Mexico City. The entire trek had been in vain.

Julia said Jacob immediately became depressed. He admitted that up until that time there had been a purpose. Then, "The life sort of went out of me," Julia quoted him. She noticed he remained devastated even 20 years later.

What came next seems surprising, but accounts for the long empty spaces in the chronological research. The life which followed was not unusual for men of that ilk in that particular time.

Frustrated by Miguel Peralta's absence, he returned to Arizona. Jacob stayed with the Pimas just existing for awhile. Remember, life in peaceful Indian settlements could be extremely rewarding to a white man. Not all white men, certainly, but a real haven to a roamer who had little desire for worldly goods. Indians accepted, never questioning or demanding or expecting anything of a man. He could sleep, eat, roam or talk at will.

Eventually, the man became restless. "I got up the gumption to go to San Francisco," he said, "which is what Jacob Weisner had wanted us both to do after we'd dug out enough gold."

The saga continued in his own words or as near as Julia could remember. "I thought I'd get a job there and forget my troubles, and then someday go back to the gold in the caches."

He got a job on the docks in 'Frisco and worked there a long time. Still unhappy and disgruntled, he returned to Arizona and filed on a piece of land in Phoenix. However, the thought of the peace he had found with the Pimas nagged at him and before long Jacob went back to them. "I lazed around for years, riding, taking long walks—living the Indian way."

One can only pity this lonely man. Was he trying to reclaim his spirit or forget a foul deed—who knows? Perhaps, those who live in a material way would never understand his actions, but anyone who has lived close to nature would agree. There was little to buy in that culture. For Jacob the search and the adventure may have been enough. He evidently abhorred city life and had no real need for possessions.

That fact was borne out by the manner in which Jacob lived later in Phoenix: a simple adobe house, chickens, a farm and very few creature comforts. The gold, after all, was probably a bit more than a day's ride away but what would he do with it? It had already cost him the life of a treasured friend whom he obviously mourned.

Eventually, the prospector did prepare for that return journey. If he was a killer he was following the premise that the murderer always returns to the scene of the crime. If not, it was just to retrieve more gold.

The weather was good in the spring of 1883. He went into the mountains on horseback tugging at the rein of a following packhorse. Along the trail there was something new. Just at the edge of the mountains a house had been built. There was a white woman there with two children with whom he visited briefly.

Waltz didn't identify them but they were the Caveness family.

Matt Caveness, a freighter for the Silver King Mine at Pinal, had constructed the house in 1879. He kept cows to supply the mines with milk and butter.

Julia, upon hearing this, remembered saying, "Grampa, ain't you afraid some cowboy'll find the mine?"

Waltz's answer is another clue to the lost mine's location. "No! The mine will never be found by any cowboy. You have to go on foot, and no cowboy's likely to do that if he can help it, and it's hard enough to find even when you know it's there," he said. He then repeated what he had said before about the location. "It's in a rough place, and you can pass within a hundred feet or so without seeing it. The gold's in a pit that the Mexicans started from the top. My partner and I just dug deeper, and it's not very far across."

Cowboys were a special breed. They had been known to hit an outcropping with a branding iron, see a piece of what could be promising quartz, stuff it into a pocket and then, completely forget where it came from. They rarely dismounted except to bed down or see to a sick animal. It wasn't laziness—they just didn't care about anything except riding fences and rounding up cows—unless, like Holmes, they got gold fever.

Waltz went on to say the white woman had seen Apaches who were always on the prowl but they had been friendly. She was still afraid of them, as was the prospector.

Later, he located the cache with no trouble. There were white men's tracks around the workings and somebody had been picking in the dump of ore. Jacob busied himself building a hasty rock wall at the mouth of the tunnel that Peralta's father had started. Then, he threw dirt against the wall to hide the rocks and left. He drew gold from one of the caches to take with him.

Here Jacob revealed his plan. "I brought the gold away from there, but the big cache is still there, I'm sure, and in the spring we'll go there together. I'll show you where the mine is, too, and then you will know all there is to know about the secret I've lived with for twenty years."

The trip was agreed upon. It was to have been in late March when the weather would be more bearable.

Again, the reader should remember that Jacob was getting old. The desert has rough extremes. It may be baking hot during the day but at night the temperature drops to extraordinary lows. Or perhaps, Jacob was concerned for Julia's discomfort outdoors at night.

Excitement was mounting in Julia's small home. At each meeting the trio planned on gear and a wagon, eagerly discussing the most minute details of their journey. By now Julia and Reiney had succumbed to a fatal disease—they had gold fever. And that fact ruined the remainder of their lives.

Was it fate or the *Curse of the Dutchman's Gold* surfacing once more, manifesting itself that spring in the form of torrential rains which fell on the eastern mountains swelling the Salt and the Verde rivers? In 1891 a great flood bore down on Phoenix. History recorded it as the most ruinous in the American Southwest.

Jim Bark, in town from his ranch, organized Mexican and Indian laborers and hired teams with Fresno scrapers. They were paid with silver from his own bank account to construct a great dike and a huge ditch to divert water away from the dirt streets of town. But, those living on the outskirts were less fortunate.

Julia, well aware of her friend's imperiled location, sent Reiney on his horse to look for the old man. Darkness had fallen before the boy arrived. Fortunately, the water was still shallow enough in that spot to allow the horse to carry Reiney to the door of the adobe. Waltz was sitting atop his bed with a blanket over his legs and a lighted candle in his hand.

Reiney told Jim Bark later that the old man's gratitude was apparent. He seemed calm but said he had taken a chill while trying to round up his chickens to put them on the roof of the coop. Reiney's quote was, "He was shivering violently as I put him onto the horse."

Later, after hot drinks and dry clothes were offered, Julia put the grateful miner to bed out in the shack behind her home. Thanks to the town fathers and men like Bark, Phoenix was safe. Jacob was not so fortunate, three days later he developed pneumonia.

The gold plagued his thoughts even then. He told Julia in a labored voice of a cache of gold hidden beneath his fireplace and asked if Reiney would go and dig it up. Then, after Reiney's return, Julia emptied the contents of the cans into a wooden candle box, covered it with an old cloth and stuffed it under Jacob's bed.

Ely said, and Reiney corroborated the story, that Jacob became delirious for several days during which he rambled. Of course, they were in constant attendance. At times when his words were more forceful they could make out what he was saying. "Where's Weisner?" he repeated over and over. "Tell Weisner to come here." And then he moaned, "I want him to know how sorry I am. I should've, should've got back in time." At other times, he would moan, "I didn't kill my partner—I didn't kill him."

Jim Bark left copious notes which have been examined thoroughly and he claimed Reiney said Waltz also said, "God forgive me I had to do it."

Of course, there was a doctor who came to attend him who also heard statements. Did Julia, in recounting the story to Sims Ely, cover for her trusted old friend? Or did Jacob only mean that he should have hurried back to camp and not stayed at Adam's Mill that extra night? No one will ever know, but from that time on a legend grew which defamed him as a murderer and Reiney's report to Jim Bark didn't help matters.

Jacob never fully recovered, instead he lingered on until October when death finally claimed him.

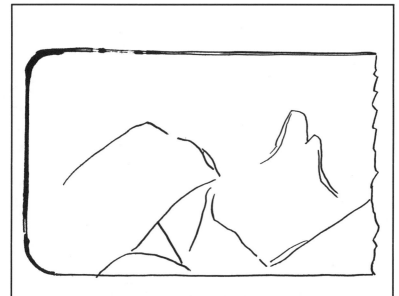

This is an exact copy of the drawing made by Jacob Waltz and given to Rhinehardt Petrasch, probably a month before his death on Oct. 25, 1891. It was made on a leaf torn from a note book, that was used for a collection of foreign stamps, some of them German.

During those last months the old man tried in vain to explain to his friends where the mine was located. More than once Julia overheard that clipped accent angrily raised against the boy. "Reiney!" he would yell, "You're not listening. You've got to pay attention. That mine is hard to find."

It is not hard to believe that Waltz was frustrated. He must have known he was going to die and wanted his friends to have the gold.

He was absolutely right—that mine was hard to find.

Meticulous research done by Tom Kollenborn produced the following facts: Julia Schaffer Thomas died in Phoenix, Arizona, on December 22, 1917 of Bright's disease. She was buried December 25, 1917 in the Jewish Cemetery. Her father's name was Kain and her mother's name was Nannie or Mannie.

Note: (Julia was Julia E. Thomas.) It is believed her middle name was Elena which the old German transposed to Helena.

Telling the truth through other people's notes becomes an awesome responsibility. It would have been a simple matter to read all three explanations then choose one to write a decent novel. Some pretty knowledgeable persons suggested simply paraphrasing the stories. Certainly—it would be simpler, but let's study the facts. Somewhere in all of these notes is the road map to the greatest lost mine in the world. Untold numbers of people have looked for and continue to look for it regardless of what is written on these pages. The loss of life over that gold has been phenomenal. It seems a duty to expose every clue in the words of those who lived it.

Ely and his partner, Jim Bark, spent an accumulated 70 years searching and took the time to write down their findings. Fortunately, they printed for posterity the adventure, their conclusions and their good wishes for others with the same goal.

Chapter 5

Bark Gets Interested in the Mine

J im Bark, destined to become a noted pioneer, was orphaned at the age of 11 in Philadelphia. Following his keen instincts, he schooled himself through reading books while selling newspapers. Later, doing construction work on railways in New Mexico, Mexico and Arizona, he made his way to Phoenix. When Bark became a land speculator and proved his financial acumen, local banks readily extended him loans at a monthly interest rate of 2 percent.

From all accounts Bark had an infectious personality and good looks. He was a big man who carried himself with determination, exuding a confident but amenable air. Before long he became an accepted civic leader. As was previously mentioned, Bark was a member of the Territorial Legislature in the upper house and assisted in pioneering the federal system of forest conservation in Washington, D.C. However, it wasn't until he was elected the first president of the Arizona Cattlegrowers Association that he met Sims Ely. That friendship was to last for the rest of their lives.

While courting his wife-to-be at Ely's home, Bark told Ely about the mine. In fact, it was Bark who coined the expression, "The Lost Dutchman's Gold Mine"; the date was 1893.

Ely later wrote that Bark had many opportunities from investors in New York to finance the search for the gold. He refused the offers saying he already had a partner, Sims Ely. It was obvious from both Bark's notes and Ely's book that the pair shared

Jim Bark

a healthy mutual respect.

Avoiding the summer months, the two men made treks through the Superstitions during the rest of the year. Jim's ranch was a three-hour ride from town over rough dirt trails. His cabin was a weathered board structure standing near the north bank of a wide, shallow canyon.

They usually rode horseback trailed by two pack animals and a cowboy escort. In spring or early fall when the rattlers were out, they packed army cots so they could sleep up off the ground. Before each trip they planned carefully, not wanting to cover too much ground. The cowboy would help them make camp—noting their location and then return to the ranch with instructions to return in no more than four days with the pack animals. Sims

*Sims Ely, 1908, at the Relief gold mine. Historical researchers
added numbers for identification.*

made a special notation of this in his book, claiming safety as
an important factor in those particular mountains. He said Adolph
Ruth, a later victim, probably would have survived had he realized
the danger of being in the Superstitions alone.

Bark and Ely traveled far afield in their searches, sometimes
hiking 15 miles up canyons and back. Bark hated heights and
it became necessary for Ely to climb alone. They took special
pains not to get hurt, yet occasionally they nearly lost their lives
slipping on shale or losing their footing near a precipice.
Systematically through the years they covered an area roughly
20 miles long and 12 miles wide in some of the world's roughest
terrain.

Ely, alluding to their finest moments, reflected on the late hours
spent by the campfire marveling over the magnificent stars in
the flawless sky, or on pre-dawn, sleepless nights when they
endlessly discussed the thorough investigation of clues. Naturally,
their search was well known. As time passed many people
approached them with testimonies of the truth as they knew it.

The men were not only having a grand adventure, they were convinced the mine existed.

After reading Bark's notes it seems safe to assume he told the truth. He enjoyed a wonderful reputation among his peers. He readily admits he never found it. He also wished good luck to all who searched for it. It seems reasonable to conclude he was an honorable man. And his notes, while adding information, make very interesting reading about a time in Arizona's history which was filled with adventure and death.

In the introduction to those notes there was a letter written by Bark which lends credence to the story.

Bark's Introductory Letter

I wish to say that the following statements are in no sense fiction; they are a collection of true stories relating to what is probably the richest deposit of gold ever worked by man. I have not included many stories which have come to me from different individuals, who would not or could not offer substantiating proof.

The reader's first thoughts will be, "If Jim Bark knows so much about where the mine is located, why doesn't he find it himself," I wish to say, that the vicinity in which I now think the mine must be, I have not nearly exhausted; that I have hunted for the mine on and off for thirty years, and I am more certain than ever that the Superstition Mountains of Arizona conceal one of the great gold mines of the world. For many years, I have dreamed of coming on the hidden opening of the mine. All the accounts agree that it is so cunningly concealed that one could walk within a few yards, or even feet, and miss it.

It is possible, of course, that someone may come upon the Dutchman by accident, but I should like to think that the fortunate wanderer who discovers this lost treasure will do so because of the material I am giving him in the following stories. They each contribute their part to the evidence that the mine exists in a definite locality in the Superstition Mountains.

Hunting the Dutchman is not for old men. Nor for old prospectors who sit on the park benches in our Western towns, and are still filled with hope, exaggeration, specimens and nicotine. They must step aside and let the younger generation hunt for the Lost Dutchman—chew their own tobacco, tell their own lies, and buy or steal their own specimens, as hunting for the Lost Dutchman is not for old men.

Someone someday will fit the parts together more successfully than we have done.

Good luck to him.

[Found in Jim Bark's notes]

JACOB WALSH

In 1891, Frank Criswell, my partner, and myself bought the Superstition Cattle Ranch from the George Marlar estate, known as the ML Ranch, and took possession early that year. My partner attended the first roundup, and as it was a very bad cattle year (on account of drought) turned the management over to me, which I retained until I sold my interest to him about the year 1912.

Scarcely had I taken charge until there were rumors and very indefinite stories about there being a very rich gold mine over the mountain, in the Superstition range, but nothing that a cattle man would pay any attention to. As I was riding the range about six miles west of the home ranch in August 1892 or 1893, I met some campers near an old well belonging to the ranch, and they proved to be a colored woman by the name of Thomas and a young man about 18 years old by the name of Rhiney Petrach, whom Mr. and Mrs. Thomas had adopted. Mr. Thomas was German, and all three spoke the German language. I had a speaking acquaintance at the time with all three as I had met them in their bakery in Phoenix. I think it was the only bakery and ice cream parlor there at that time. It was generally known in Phoenix that Thomas had run away with another woman, and that Mrs. Thomas No. 1 and the boy Petrach were still running the bakery. So I was somewhat surprised to meet them camped near the Superstition mountain, as it was very hot and an extremely desolate country to camp in. I asked them why they were camped there, and she replied that they were out on a vacation. I invited them to come up to the house as they at least would have shade. She replied that they were going back in a short time, so I rode on up the canyon, following their buggy tracks, and they had gone up the canyon toward the Superstition mountains, as far as it was possible to go with a horse and buggy, and much farther than I thought was possible. At that time, I did not know that they had closed shop in Phoenix for good, but such proved to be the case. Afterward, Mrs. Thomas and the boy were frequently seen by the cowboys, camped first at one water hole, then another, over in the main Superstition Range, but always with saddle horses and pack animals. One day, they came by the ranch, and there were four in the party. The other two proved to be the brother, Herman and the father of the two boys or men, known as old man Petrach, and that they had just arrived from Montana. Shortly after that, the party came by the ranch and stopped over night. There seemed to be more or less dissension amongst them, and Rhiney told me that they had been looking for a gold mine but could find no trace of it; that he had written his father and brother in regard to it, and they had concluded that Rhiney and Mrs. Thomas knew nothing of mining or the mountains, and as the men were both prospectors, they decided that they had better go to Phoenix, and then go up in the Superstition mountains and find it. Rhiney said that they had made a thorough search and that he was going to quit, as he and Mrs. Thomas had blown in all the money they had and they were all getting pretty grouchy, and that if I would say that I would do what was right with them in case I found the mine by his description and information he would tell me the story and answer any questions that he could; that as I was going to be riding the mountains, I might unravel the story and possibly find the mine; that he knew it was there, and he believed it to be the richest gold mine in the world. I told him all right, and to go ahead with his story. This was in the evening.

He said that in the late 80s there was a Raymond excursion going to the Pacific coast over the Southern Pacific railroad and they stopped over at old Maricopa and took the stage for a visit to Phoenix, and among them was a soda fountain manufacturer

Jim Bark's Ranch, Pinal County, AZ., later owned by Barkley.

who sold to Thomas an ebony and marble fountain for twenty-five hundred dollars, five hundred dollars down. When the first payment came due, Thomas instead of making the payment skipped out with a white woman, and as far as Rhiney knew had never been heard from. There was an old German who had forty acres of school land and some chickens, and who had often sold his eggs to the bakery. He would frequently have a chat in German with Mr. and Mrs. Thomas and the boy, so when Helena (first name of Mrs. Thomas) realized that Thomas had actually skipped out with another woman, she went crying up to Old Jake's adobe house just east of Phoenix, and told him that she did not know what she would do, as she owed a whole lot of money, and that Thomas had taken all there was belonging to them with him when he skipped; and that they owed two thousand dollars on the fountain and quite a flour bill, and several others, and that she had no money to pay them with. This was early in 1891. Old Jake stepped to the door of his one-room adobe, placed one foot in front of the other, handed Helena an old pick and told her to dig there. She did so, unearthing an oyster can in which was about eight hundred dollars in gold nuggets. Old Jake said, "Take it Helena; this will do you until I can come down to the bakery and we will go over the bills

95

together." Helena replied, "No, no Jake, I don't know when I can repay you." And he said, "Now, now, don't worry as I have fifty more of these buried around." So she took it, and paid some of her smaller bills; and that when she and Jake went through the affairs, they found that there were some seventeen hundred dollars of bills, beside the two thousand on the fountain. They both said that Jake squared all of the bakery accounts. After Thomas skipped, old Jake was quite a frequenter at the bakery and was familiar with the earnings. One evening sitting out on the porch of the house, he told them about having a rich gold mine in the Superstition mountains, and that there was no need of their working so hard for just a living, and that if they would listen he would tell them where it was and how he became the owner.

The Dutch Jake Story

His partner, Jacob Wiser, and himself were prospecting in the sixties in the state of Sonora, Mexico, and one evening they came to a ranch and asked a Mexican whom they saw if they and their burros could camp there for the night. He said he did not know, but that he would go and see the Don. He returned and told them that the Don wanted to know if they were Americans. He had told the Don that they did not talk like Americans but were white men. "Well, tell them they can camp and for both of them to come up and see me this evening at seven." Which they did. The Don asked them what they were doing, and they said, "Prospecting." He asked if they had found anything, and they told him they had not. He wanted to know if they were Americans, and they said they were naturalized citizens. The Don said that he was getting an expedition together to go up into the United States to a mine that had been in possession of their family for several generations, a grant of sole right to Miguel Peralta (who was his grandfather) and his heirs, to a mine in certain territory, describing the corners, three of which were natural, and the other was a monument of stone laid in mortar of mud (which is the same in Mexican) ten feet square and eight feet high, and built like a pyramid. The three natural corners are easily found, but the fourth corner he had been informed by an Apache Indian, was torn down by them, and it must be so as it was never found.

He wanted some Americans in his party, as his title to the mine was simply a sole right to mine within certain described boundaries and not a deed of conveyance and perpetuity; that it was not recognized by the United States; that if they would go with him he, Peralta, would give them a third of what he took out. They agreed to go, and they went up into the Superstition mountains, had a brush with the Apache Indians on the way out, and two were wounded. Upon their arrival at the Peralta ranch in Sonora, their share of the spoils was a little over thirty thousand dollars. I failed to mention that there were twenty-one in the party (eighteen peons). Don Peralta proposed to give them a bill of sale to the mine for their share of the gold. They accepted the bill of sale and came back to the mine. As they were about to camp, they heard some one breaking rock up the canyon. So they took their guns, a double barrel muzzle loader shot gun, loaded with buckshot, the other a muzzle loading Sharp's rifle, and crawled up to within sight of the tunnel, and there were two naked men (all but a gee string) whom they thought were Indians. They each selected his man and fired. Both were killed, but when they went up to them, they discovered that they were two of the peons that were in the party that came up on the previous trip. They buried them, mined about three weeks and went back to Peralta. They found that Peralta had been to Mexico City during their absence, had been gambling heavily and was in debt. He asked them how much gold they had, and they told him about sixty thousand dollars. He said he needed money badly and if they would let him have the sixty thousand that he would give them a mortgage on his ranch, with good interest. After talking it over, they decided that they did not want a mortgage, but would take his note, as they said they could return to the mine and get more. So they took the note and struck out again for the mine. After their arrival there, they concluded that they were going to run out of grub, so Jacob Walsh took the burros and went down to Adamsville (just below Florence) where there was an adobe grist mill and a kind of general store kept for the Pima Indians; in fact, a kind of trader's store. Walsh said he was gone three or four days. Right there, the first doubt about the story entered my mind about his telling the truth, as I could not understand how a miner having made two trips to the this same deposit just previously, should go in there with a shortage of grub, but the explanation to this comes later on in the story.

Upon his return to the mine, he found his partner, Jacob Wiser, stripped naked and his new hickory shirt hanging on a bush nearby with his Masonic pin sticking to it. Doubt No. 2. I never knew an Apache Indian to overlook any kind of a shirt, much less a new hickory shirt. The camp in general was shot up and destroyed; that the handle of the frying pan was broken off and three bullet holes through the pan and many other utensils destroyed by bullets.

Doubt No. 3, for if there was one thing in the world that an Apache was careful about, and sparing and jealous of, it was ammunition, and for them to waste it on frying pans and coffee pots was entirely out of the question in my mind. He said that he buried his partner, walled up the tunnel, rolled dirt and rock over it and took the frying pan without a handle with the bullet holes in it; *that there were mountain peaks just west and above the mine, and that he placed this frying pan with four small rocks on it on the center peak, and that if we would go down the peak due east, we would find the mine. The center of four was another stumbling block.* I have unravelled all the other discrepancies but this one still remains, and the only solution to it is that he may have said three; *that no cowboy could ever find it, which I take it to mean that one cannot ride a burro to it, or within sight of it*; and for some reason, *there is an interruption in the trail going to it, as a cowboy will go anywhere that a trail leads.*

Jacob also said that *no prospector would find it*, which I take to mean that it is not a mineral formation. In fact, he said it was not, and that *he had never seen anything like it and that it was very difficult to find; that the trail that went over the mountain to the mine was monumented with* two little rocks placed upon a larger rock, or some other conspicuous place.

He would always start the subject of the mine whenever he found Rhiney or Helena idle and up at the house, and appeared provoked when he thought they were not paying attention. He would chide them and say, "When I am gone, you will wish you had listened to me."

Jake was about eighty-six years old and evidently was not expecting to live long. In early March, 1891, he told them that he did not think they could find the way to the mine, and that he had better get a couple of ponies and a couple of burros, a wagon and some grub, and go with them as far as the new board house, where there was a woman and three children, and that was as far as he could go. From there on, it would have to be on horseback, and he thought he could show them the trail over the mountain looking from the house, and they must wear their oldest clothes because the brush was bad.

Old Jake said that he had been to the mine but once since he left it and came to Phoenix and that was fourteen years after he walled up the tunnel, and that everything was just as he had left it, and he did not disturb anything.

The reason I am so sure he was referring to the Bark and Criswell ranch is that Matt Caveness and his wife built the big board house in 1877, and took his four draft horses as he had a contract to haul ore from the Silver King mine to Pinal where they were building the mill some five miles from the mine. Mrs. Caveness and the three children stayed at the ranch and ran a dairy. She sold butter at Pinal and the King, some twenty miles away, and got as high as a dollar a pound. As there was no other woman or children, or board house in that entire country, there is not much doubt as to the new board house he was referring to. Also the trail over into the Superstition mountains was monumented in just such a manner as old Jacob described. At this board house, the wagon road ended. Mrs. Caveness told many of the cattle men that she frequently sold flour to the Apache Indians, and that they always paid her in gold nuggets; and that one time, an Indian came to the house about ten o'clock in the morning and asked her for some flour, saying that he would go over the big mountain and get the gold. She refused the flour, telling him to get the gold first. He rode up the trail over the mountains and returned before sundown with the gold. Will Whitlow, a neighbor cattleman, was present at times when she was selling to the Indians, and he said that she sold a milk pan full of flour for about ten dollars worth of gold. She told the same thing to many others.

Jake finally got his outfit together, loaded the wagon with grub, and they were planning on starting the next day, but that night the great flood came down Salt River and in the morning water was covering all of lower Phoenix. Helena told Rhiney that he had better go and see how old Jake was situated. When the boy got in sight of Jake's house, water was all around it. When he got to the house, he found Jake standing up on his bed in about six inches of water. The boy took him on his back to Helena's house, and finally Jake with all his effects moved there and stayed until he died in the fall of 1891. He lived several months after the flood but was never able to go to the mountains. He could sit out on the porch at times, and when he did he would point to the Superstition mountains and say, "The mine lies right over there."

Among his things that were moved over to Helena's house was a soap box, very heavy, with leather hinges, a hasp and a lock, which he always insisted should not be opened, but was to remain under his cot. Everyone thought it contained ore, but no one knew. When Jake was passing away, he kept murmuring "God forgive me; I had to do it," and then he would repeat it, and those around him supposed he had killed his partner, Jacob Wiser. There was an old prospector by the name of old Germany, who would drop in and see Jake, and Jake would say, "Tell him to go out; I don't want him here." He gave Rhiney three small pieces of ore and said they were from the mine. Rhiney got hard up, pounded two of the pieces up, washed the gold out and got some eight dollars for it. Jake died without any of them going to the mountain to look for the mine. When they went to the funeral, the soap box disappeared, and Helena and Rhiney each suspected the other with making away with it, but both were innocent, and *it is not necessary to the story to mention the name of the guilty party, so I will pass it.*

It was some time before Helena and Rhiney could dispose of the bakery and go look for the mine. Their first trip was the time I mentioned in the first part of this story. Rhiney told me that the first time Helena and he went over the mountain to look for the mine, she got lost on top of a mountain, and as it was sundown she became frantic; that there quite a number of the dry rattle weed up there and that she got up on a large rock and stopped there all night. She carried a small 32 revolver and a box of cartridges. As dark was overtaking her, the rattle weeds began to rattle and she mistook them for rattlesnakes; so she stayed on the boulder all night and fired all her cartridges away at the snakes.

This practically is the story I got out of Rhiney that evening, and by morning, I had a list of forty-one questions that I asked him. Some he answered "yes" or "no," and some he did not know. I kept the questions, changed them about and asked him the same questions again and wrote the answers, about three months after questioning him the first time, and he only varied in one question; and that was the time Jake said it took him to go to Adamsville and back. The first time it was three or four days; the last time, it was four days. At that time, it was quite important, but as the story unravelled it made no difference.

Rhiney made several trips with the party after that. Sometimes Herman was off on his own hook, but the old man Petrach was always one of the party. Sometime after Rhiney had told me the story, Helena, the old man, and Rhiney came over from the mountain on horses that were miserably poor and one that they were packing. They came to the ranch about sundown and asked if they could get some hay and grain for their horses and something to eat for themselves. They said that a dollar and seventy-five cents was all the money they had and that they would like to keep that so as to buy some grub and hay in Mesa, some thirty-five miles towards Phoenix in the Salt River Valley. I told them they would have to do their own cooking, as we had had our supper, and that the horse feed was down in the grainery, and for them to help themselves which they did. They stayed all night and struck out in the morning for Mesa.

They camped there that night, and during the night the handbag that Helena always kept in her possession disappeared. *Who got it, or where it went, I do not wish to say.* The handbag contained Jake's parchment map of the mine, and how to get to it, Peralta's note to the two Jakes for sixty thousand dollars, bill of sale to the two Jakes to the mine and Jake Walsh's naturalization certificate.

101

I saw no more of them for a long time, but Pete showed up shortly after that, and I hired him to keep the water holes clean, attend to the pumping, and do other odd jobs, but not as a cow hand . . .

Now in regard to the monumented trail: I have followed it over the mountain without difficulty, and then the monuments could not be found for about two miles, when we found them along a trail where cattle did not travel, thence over a divide into the horse country, where the monuments failed us again, but led us to a much more significant feature of the story: that is, the cut mesquite timber. Helena and Rhiney said that Jake told them that there were *two pits at the mine about 75 feet deep and a like distance across the top*; that they were lined with mesquite wood and would drop about six feet, then an offset of about a foot, and so on down to the bottom. Upon every offset, there would be a toe ladder, a stick of timber with notches cut in it that the peons would climb by placing their toes in the notches, taking hold of the timber with their hands and finally reaching the top with a rawhide sack on their backs and a strap around their foreheads, the sack filled with ore. It really was astonishing to see how fast men who were used to that kind of mining could come up from the bottom with a load of about one hundred pounds. Now, those pits took considerable mesquite, and we positively have found where they were cut, and they could not have been cut for any other purpose that we can conceive, and they were all cut with an ax, a tool that Apache Indians never used. The cut timber must have gone down, as the cutting is on top of the mountain and covers quite a large area. We have been working on the cut timber for several years; and we have found where they had quite a camp at one time, just to cut and pack the wood. They must have left it in a hurry, as we found a lot of small horseshoes (new), several kegs, gone to staves and hoops, as there is no water there, and other evidences of camp. Now, we think we know very nearly where the wood left the mesa and that will be our next attack this winter. Jake also told them that at times Juaquin Murietta, the bandit with his gang, would join with the Peralta outfit and come to the Superstition mountains and to the Peralta camp as a mutual protection; and that at the camp *they had a Mexican race track,* and that Murietta's outfit would run horses against Peralta's. He said they would skin the Peraltas out of all the money they had, and that Murietta had a silver mine somewhere beyond and they would move on to this mine for a load of silver ore. I have undoubtedly found that camp and the race track.

I forgot to state that upon the death of Jake, the ground around his house was most thoroughly dug up, but nothing found.

The foregoing is practically the story of Jacob Walsh, with the wheat separated from the chaff as near as it is humanly possible to do.

These notes are a repetition of the story Sims extracted from Julia in the early 1900s. It is necessary to include them given the fact that they came from two different sources but are essentially the same. Remember, Reiney had left Phoenix before Sims arrived. His interviews with the lady were conducted at another time and place.

Jim Bark, on the other hand, had repeatedly questioned Reiney. Reiney must have known of Bark's reputation among the townspeople of Phoenix and saw him as his only hope of ever acquiring some of the now famous Dutchman's ore. Bark knew the terrain, had money and cowboys at his disposal and was keenly interested in the mine's location.

The comparison of all of these interviews allows a peek into the past through a relatively clean window.

Chapter 6

Jacob Weisner

Dr. John Walker was duly noted in Western lore, and although he was an early California immigrant who was educated there as a physician and surgeon, he was among the first to volunteer for the California Column. Walker and his cohorts were sent to Arizona and New Mexico to replace Union Troops withdrawn from desert garrisons in the War Between the States.

Serving as a master of a wagon train, the young soldier transported wheat and flour from Pima farms along the Gila River to posts in both territories and even into Texas, making friends all along the trail.

During his tour of duty, Walker became extremely ill and decided to take up residence in an adobe house in a friendly Pima village. After a long recovery, he made good use of his medical skills both in Pima camps and with the equally passive Maricopa tribes. Both tribes were farmers who also raised cattle. Since they had been Christianized soon after the Spanish conquest, they readily accepted the comfort of a white man's medicine. Before long Walker had become a mentor, healer and friend who gave unselfishly of himself.

Among his Pima nurses during his long illness was a beautiful Indian maiden named Churga. The two fell in love and were later married in a typical Indian wedding ceremony. That union pro-

Walker Helped Advance
The Friendly Pima Tribe

ONE CANNOT STUDY THE history of the Pima Indians without noting the influence several white men had upon their lives, particularly from the time of the great migration through their country of the gold seekers on their way, in 1849 and later, to the California gold fields—or just to California.

One of the most interesting of these men was John D. Walker. His name became particularly well known after his death, because his heirs and other contestants kept up a costly and long, drawn out litigation for the wealth he had acquired through ownership of the famous Vekol silver mine southwest of Casa Grande.

The story of this unusual character's activities and association with the friendly tribe of Pima Indians is a most interesting one. In the eyes of many chroniclers of the later-day history of the tribe, he is credited with doing as much for their advancement as any white man of the period, unless it be the

Rev. Charles Cook who established a mission among them in the early 1870s.

BORN IN ILLINOIS in 1840 and said to have been part Indian, John D. Walker went to California as a young man and was living there when the Civil War broke out in 1861. Being strongly anti-slavery, he joined the California Volunteers, who were organized early in the war to take the place of the Indian fighting soldiers withdrawn from Arizona and New Mexico.

Made an officer, he was in charge of one or more of the wagon trains accompanying the Volunteers into Arizona.

One of his first duties was hauling supplies overland from San Diego and Los Angeles to Ft. Yuma and to interior forts, or camps, that were being established.

When he arrived at the Pima villages along the Gila River, he found the Confederates under Captain Hunter had taken possession of part of the wheat and corn the Volunteers had bought from the Pimas and had destroyed

First part of article published in Arizona Days and Ways by Roscoe C. Willson.

duced a daughter named Juana. The doctor adored the child and lovingly called her Juanita. The father and daughter were very close. Within 10 years of her birth Churga died and Juanita moved to the center of Dr. Walker's life. That little girl became another factor in the Dutchman's saga.

Indians had very little use for precious metals. In time, and to repay the good doctor, the Pimas directed him to a valuable silver deposit which became known as the Vekol mine. That acquisition eventually made the man one of the richest in the Arizona territory.

Walker had come to regard all of the Pimas as his family; he spent over $500,000 of the mine's proceeds improving living conditions for the Pimas.

The Apaches were still on the warpath. Frequent raids on peaceful Pima camps to steal livestock and food caused constant fear and much loss of life. The Army was called upon to put an end to the raids. Walker became the leader of a troop of Indian soldiers who were entreated to go into the Superstitions to wipe out the savages.

The last big battle took place on a precipice where defeated Apache warriors leaped to their deaths rather than be taken prisoner. The ledge ultimately became infamous and was forever known as Apache Leap. Walker gained much respect in the territory by refusing to turn over the remaining prisoners to Indians who wanted to torture them for revenge. Instead, he marched them to Fort McDowell. That battle ended Apache raids outside the Superstitions forever.

Walker returned to his home and practice and a peaceful life among the Indians.

Six years later in the fall of 1871, a wounded man struggled out of the Superstitions. Two Pima Indians found Jacob Weisner and brought him to Dr. Walker's home.

According to Sims Ely, Dr. Walker's story was as follows: "I'm terribly wounded, doctor," Weisner gasped.

Indian women who worked for the physician prepared food. A stimulant was administered and after the patient was put to bed, Walker removed the man's clothing and bathed him. There was a festering wound in both the upper left arm and shoulder. The considerable bleeding had stopped and an examination proved no major artery or vein had been damaged.

Weisner looked ghostly. Pale from loss of blood, suffering and exposure he nonetheless was able to choke out that he was the victim of an Apache arrow. His was indeed a tale of horror, for in his agony he had torn the spear out of his own flesh.

Weisner was given drugs throughout the night. By morning Dr. Walker knew his patient had pneumonia and probably wouldn't live.

The doctor patiently began to question the man by asking first if he had relatives in Arizona. The answer was, "No. All my relatives live in Germany and they are just cousins. My parents died. I haven't any brothers or sisters."

The doctor continued, "Any friends in Arizona or elsewhere in this country?"

"I had a friend," Weisner answered. "My partner. But the Apaches got him the same way they got me. Why you askin' me these questions? Am I goin' to die?"

Walker was as reassuring as he could be, but admitted Weisner was very sick.

Weisner seemed consoled saying, "It's all right Doc, if I don't get up. I got the feelin' I'm going to die, anyway."

Walker said the man then fell silent for a long time and then said, "When the Indians brought me in, did I have a sack with me?"

The doctor answered, "Why, yes. It's still here over there on the floor."

Weisner asked him to get it.

The doctor said later it was an ordinary bag about the size of a flour sack. Handing it to the sick man, Walker watched him open it exposing a few toilet articles and a piece of rawhide.

Dr. Walker assured him that was all he had asking, "Ought there to have been anything else?"

"No! Left 'em behind—my rifle and revolver and anythin' else that weighed anythin'—at the last water hole. But this," he went on, after picking up the piece of rawhide, "this is a map. It's a map my partner and I got in Mexico. Shows the route from Sonora to a mine in them mountains to the north. One of the great gold mines of the world. If I die, I want you to have the map and the mine."

Weisner paused, studied the rawhide and then began to interpret the map.

Dr. Walker listened close, and the details remained in his mind long years afterward.

"My partner and I went to the mine first with the Mexican owner. His name was Don Miguel Peralta. We went to it as partners all three of us. Don Miguel wanted fightin' men with him, and my partner and I were soldiers in the Confederate Army. And we'd saved Don Miguel's life in a brawl in Mexico. We were to have one half of the gold we took out, Don Miguel the other half.

"We took peons with us. Any number of 'em, all well-armed. And we brought away about sixty thousand dollars. Then Don Miguel asked us to let him have most of our share. He needed money bad, and he gave us a paper that said we were to have the mine for ourselves as long as we wanted it. He was only doin' what he had a right to do—the old man, Don Miguel's father, was killed at the mine a few years ago, and Don Miguel had neither wife nor children. And now, it'll be your mine if I die, for my partner is gone."

Walker said Weisner's eyes drifted away. He was silent for a long time.

The doctor remained patient and waited silently.

Eventually, Weisner began again. "My partner and I went back to the mine alone. After we'd worked it for a number of weeks, our mule destroyed most of our provisions, and my partner undertook to come out to the Adams Mill for supplies. He never got back. I expected him on the fourth day. And then, on the mornin' of the fifth day, when the Apaches jumped me, I knew they'd killed my partner first.

"Apaches got all the animals 'cept one horse. I rode him a few miles, but the goin' was slow, and then their arrows stopped him. I got one in the arm, but I kept on goin'. Runnin', then stoppin' behind rocks to fire my rifle at 'em. They were afraid to come too close, and at last they turned back. I made for the first water hole on the desert I knew about."

He said he was suffering a terrible thirst by the time he reached the water hole, and the wound pained him unbearably. Sometime before he got to the water he guessed he must have become delirious, because it was then he tore out the arrow. He stayed at the water hole for most of the day, and then, in a moment of clarity, he realized that he had lost his canteen and would have to make it across the desert without any more water. He made it to the river somehow and the Pimas found him and brought him to Dr. Walker.

At this point the doctor could see Jacob was exhausted and cautioned his patient not to talk anymore. Then, he told the dying man he would administer medicine to make him sleep.

All through the long night Walker sat diligently but helplessly beside Jacob's bed. By morning the patient was delirious. The doctor could only ease his suffering and hope. On the fourth day after his arrival in the village, Weisner died.

Dr. Walker instructed the Indians to make a coffin. He then saw to it the man had a decent burial in the graveyard down by the river where other white travelers who had had similar fates were buried.

By now the physician was intrigued. However, he knew gold mines never ran very deep—perhaps the ore had played out. Of course, the Apaches still roamed the canyons and Dr. Walker was a hated enemy. Life in the Pima camp was too sweet to risk death or worse, possible capture at the hands of fiends who enjoyed torture. But, most of all he thought of his little girl, Juanita, whose mother had died. She needed him.

Was it fate which allowed Jacob to escape, be shot, risk dying of thirst in the burning desert—all to tell his story? Whatever the reason, the curse had claimed another life. The legend lived on

The ominous Superstition Mountains.

and now there was a map.

This matter brings up an interesting point. Weisner never named his friend. That must be the reason no one ever put it together until by some quirk of fate Tom Weedin entered the picture.

Chapter 7

The Map

By 1911 Arizona was preparing for statehood. Thomas F. Weedin, editor of the *Florence Blade* newspaper, had decided to run for governor and was busy gathering his forces.

The territory was buzzing. All the men who had been active in local matters and whose names had come to prominence must surely have been preening their feathers to become legislators. Jim Bark would be one of them.

By now Sims Ely had achieved notoriety as a newsman in Phoenix. Tom Weedin dropped into the newspaper office to see Sims. Naturally, the two men had a lot in common due to their mutual businesses. Sims received him cordially and they began to talk about the race and Tom's upcoming candidacy. After their business was concluded Tom mentioned that he had seen Jim Bark earlier in the day at the train station. He then went on to say that he knew of Sims' and Jim's mutual interest in a lost gold mine.

The newsman was immediately puzzled until Tom said in a lowered voice that there was bad blood between Jim Bark and himself for a long time and it was over political differences. The candidate continued saying that he knew something about that mine which he had been meaning to pass on for a long time but had just not gotten to it.

By that time Jim Bark had been tracking the mystery for 15

or 16 years and it was a well-known fact that Jim believed the mine existed.

Being married to a Dutchman hunter, this author has some idea of what must have been going on Sims Ely's mind at that point. Imagine, for the first time he knew that Weisner actually existed and Julia's story was true. And, right in front of him sat a man who had a map. So near and yet, so far.

Tom said in a matter-of-fact way, "I've got that tracing among my papers in Florence. I'll be home again before the end of the campaign. I'll find it and send it to you." Tom continued, "On one trip I made to the Bark Ranch years ago, I saw that the landmarks there fitted in with the map. And near there is Miner's Needle, which I decided was the pichacho that's mentioned. You're welcome to the map, I hope it leads you and Jim Bark to the mine."

It is incumbent upon the reader to realize that all of the mountains, canyons, buttes, washes and streams in the Superstitions were nameless at that time. Apache Leap had been named from the battle, Soldier's Trail from the Cavalry, Miner's Needle and a few more. There were few maps in existence but one is included herein which Tom Kollenborn found in an atlas published in 1890. Bob Corbin has a copper territorial map in his office in the State Capitol, a gift from the Department of Public Safety.

The territory was rough and essentially unknown on paper. All the names used today came about after events which were yet to come. And, as strange as it may seem, to this day Jacob's name is not on one of them. Also there was an earthquake within the range in the late 1800s which many claim covered the mine, but that is not true—it was found after that event. However, if one is systematic in researching these stated clues, they must remember that rivers do change course. And, the reservation which is referred to as being on the map was of a migratory Indian population which may have moved for any number of reasons. True Dutchman hunters spend a lot of time comparing old, hardly factual maps with the exact ones in existence today.

Tom Weedin kept his word; he searched his house trying to

find the map. His wife helped, suggesting he must have given it away to some prospector and had forgotten the incident.

Years later Miss Jennie Weedin, who Sims referred to as Tom's brilliant daughter, became a close friend of the newsman. After their friendship cemented they naturally talked about the map which her father had. She confided to Sims that her mother had destroyed it to keep Tom out of the dreaded Superstitions.

[This researcher was aghast when she read that bit of evidence. It can only be likened to the time yours truly taped over the second half of the Super Bowl on the VCR. One of my husband's lawyers called me from the office the next day to say his staff of legal minds had researched the matter, and they claimed it was grounds for divorce in the Arizona Statutes. I shudder to think what would have happened if I had destroyed the map to the Lost Dutchman gold mine.]

The curse seemed to have progressed as expected. No one knows if Dr. Walker had decided to search for the Dutchman's mine, but Dr. John Walker, the owner of the lost map, lost his mind and died in an asylum in Napa County, California, in 1894 or 1895.

The rest of his story has little to do with the map or the gold, but it is so astounding it begs to be told.

The beautiful Juanita, by rights a rich woman, was perhaps the most eligible young woman in the territory at that time. Ultimately, the doctor's heirs descended on Arizona and filed a lawsuit claiming the Indian wedding ceremony had not been legal. A tumultuous court battle followed during which Juanita was declared an illegitimate child who was also a half-breed and, therefore, definitely not entitled to the Vekol mine or any of her father's worldly possessions. She returned to the tribe, went into seclusion and never spoke to a white man again.

Doctor Walker's effects were absorbed by the heirs and the map was lost forever.

Sims supposedly had Tom Weedin draw the map from memory and there is one which Bark had with his papers (it appears within this chapter), but Bark never found the mine.

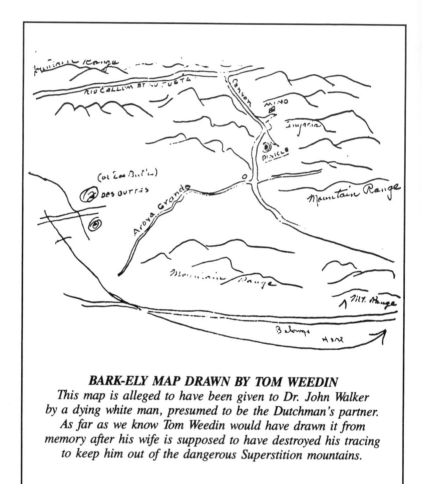

BARK-ELY MAP DRAWN BY TOM WEEDIN
*This map is alleged to have been given to Dr. John Walker
by a dying white man, presumed to be the Dutchman's partner.
As far as we know Tom Weedin would have drawn it from
memory after his wife is supposed to have destroyed his tracing
to keep him out of the dangerous Superstition mountains.*

So far we can attest to the deaths of Don Peralta, the Mexican peons who were shot by Waltz and Weisner, Phipps, Jacob himself, his partner Weisner, Reiney's father and younger half-brother, and Dr. Walker. There were more deaths to come; the Grim Reaper stalked the mine.

The Weisner Story as Told by Jim Bark
Dr. Walker was the only known white man to have been taken into and made one of the Pima Indian tribe. He married an

Indian and raised a family, and was quite an influential member of the tribe. He was well thought of by both the whites and Pimas. His greatest, and really close white friend was Hon. Tom Weedin who lived at Florence some thirty miles up the Gila River. Weedin was the owner and publisher of the Florence paper, and frequently on Sundays would go down and have an all day's visit with Walker.

One day, I think it was the year 1916, I met Hon. Tom Weedin at the railroad depot in Humboldt, Yavapai County, Arizona. He was campaigning for the nomination of governor of Arizona on the Democratic ticket. Our present governor-elect Hunt was then his opponent. We shook hands. He then remarked, "Have you a few minutes to spare, Jim?" I had, and we sat on the edge of the station platform, as it would be some little time before the train came along going to Prescott. He started the conversation by saying, "I hear that you have been looking for an old gold mine in the Superstition mountains, called locally the 'Lost Dutchman Mine.'" I said, "Yes, and I spent considerable money hunting for it." "Well, I believe it is there, and if I give you any information that will assist you in finding it, will you do what is right by me." I told him that I certainly would, and he told me the following:

That one Sunday while visiting Walker and after the usual greetings, Walker burst forth by saying, "Tom, I think we will both be rich very soon: that a few days ago a couple of Pima Indians came down from Blackwater, a trading station about twenty miles above Walkers on the Indian reservation, and said that a white man came in there last night on foot; that he was sick, and what should they do with him. Walker asked if he had a horse, and they said he had not. "Is he an American?" They said they did not think he was, although he was a white man. He talked funny and not like an American. "Do you think he can ride a horse?" They did not know, but would try him. "Well, go back and bring him down here."

They did so, and when the man arrived, Walker found that he had a very high fever. He put him on a cot that had already been prepared for him in one of his adobe houses. He told Walker that he was a German and that his name was so-and-so; the name

117

Tom Weedin, his wife and daughter, Jennie.

was entirely forgotten by Walker. In fact, he paid no attention to the name; he couldn't think of it. A gunny sack about one-quarter full of clothes, etc. was with the German. The next morning, Walker visited his patient, took his temperature, and told him if he wished to leave any word for anyone he had better do it soon. He then asked Walker if that meant he was going to die. Walker told him that if he could not break his fever within the next few hours, it was doubtful he could pull through.

The German then said, "Please hand me that gunny sack (referring to the sack that he brought with him). When it was given to him, he reached in and drew out a small tobacco sack nearly filled with gold nuggets, and said, "Here, take this. I hope this will pay you for your trouble and my burial." Walker took it. In the meantime, the German had dropped the gunny sack to the floor. He then asked Walker to get a round roll out for him, saying, "That is a map to the richest gold mine I ever knew of, and, I believe in the world." It was a piece of parchment with blue tracings, and the descriptions in Spanish. "It is an old Mexican mine, worked by the Mexicans, on and off, for many years. The mine is located in the Superstition mountains, and has a tunnel and two pits. It was being worked by my partner and me and was owned by us, but the Apache Indians jumped us, and they got him, but I managed to give them the slip and get away, though I guess not for long, as I think I worked too hard in getting away."

The old German died of pneumonia that night, and Walker buried him on the reservation. Weedin asked Walker if he had the map, and he handed it to Weedin. They poured over it, and finally Weedin suggested that he take the map to his office in Florence and make a tracing of it. He had some tracing paper there, and then they would each have a map. After making the tracing, he returned the original map to Walker, and they agreed to keep it quiet until they could go together and locate the mine, but when one was ready, the other could not get away, and so it went until a Pima Indian one day showed Walker the Vekol mine, which was just an undisturbed vein at that time, but very rich in silver. From then on, Walker was busy developing the Vekol, building a mill, making roads, sinking shafts, running tunnels, etc., and by the way, Walker cleaned up about a half million dollars out of the Vekol. Neither Weedin or Walker ever went to look for the Lost Dutchman mine.

After hearing this story from Weedin, I wrote to Sims Ely, Sr., in Phoenix, who was interested with me in looking for the Lost Dutchman mine, told him the story and for him to get busy and get the tracing. Weedin had told me he felt sure he had it. Ely went to Florence and saw Weedin, who, after searching through his papers, remembered that while he was making a tracing of the map, his wife came into the office and asked him what he was doing. He told her the story as he had it from Walker and that he was making a tracing of the map. Mrs. Weedin was very much disturbed, and said that he was not going over in the Superstition mountains, as the Apache Indians were still there killing every white man they ran across. She insisted upon taking possession of the tracing, and when she left the office she had it with her. Weedin thought the tracing must be at the house, but Mrs. Weedin, after looking through her papers denied having it. Shortly after, Mrs. Weedin died and Weedin and his daughter searched thoroughly through her papers but failed to find the tracing.

Weedin then told Ely that perhaps he had given it to some prospector, but he did not think so. He then said that he felt sure he could draw a map from memory that would be almost correct, if not absolutely so, as the details of the map were so thoroughly impressed upon his mind. Ely then told him to draw one as he remembered it, and in a very few minutes Weedin drew a memory copy of the map, which certainly pertained to the Superstition mountains. As he never was there, it should be fairly correct. We have the map he drew for us, and two of three letters which he wrote to us about the map and trail.

It is my belief that the German who gave Walker the map was none other than Jacob Wiser, Old Jack Walsh's partner, who Jacob Walsh said he found at the mine dead, stripped naked and his new hickory shirt hanging on a bush nearby, upon Jacob Walsh's return with grub from Adamsville.

First, it looks unreasonable that two men knowing where they were going and about how long they were going to stay and

—— SPECIAL SECTION ——

In the Kollenborn/Corbin collection are over 100 lost treasure maps of which the following are the most appropriate to this research.

While Bob Corbin was County Attorney in the 60s, he became acquainted with Arnold Ortiz, a bailiff in the Maricopa County Courthouse. Arnold knew of Bob's interest in lost treasure and told him the following story: "When my father was young he hired an old Indian who came by looking for work on our Chandler farm. The pair became great friends. Later, after the friendship cemented, he offered my father a letter and a map to a mine in the Superstitions. The Indian said years before he was hunting near Weaver's Needle when he came upon two white men. They started shooting at him. He fired back and one of them fell; the other one ran away. After it was safe the Indian approached to see if the man was wounded. He was dead. The Indian then searched his pockets. The letter and the map were on the body." For years following that incident Arnold's father made trips into the Superstitions with some prospecting partners from Mesa, looking for the mine, but they were unable to locate it. During one of those trips, the map and the letter disappeared. Mr. Ortiz never knew what happened to it.

By 1986 after Bob Corbin became Attorney General, he called Arnold. Bob mentioned a map called the Ortiz map which had been given to him by Tom Kollenborn. He asked Arnold to come by his office to take a look at it. Arnold Ortiz smiled when Corbin handed it to him saying, "Do you mind turning it upside down, Bob? I was a young boy when my father used to pore over that map and I would stand with my nose table high on the other side. I memorized it upside down." After studying the document for a few moments, Arnold said there were some lines missing. He drew them in lightly with a pencil. He also said that his father's map was drawn on a piece of leather and this map must have been copied from it.

Bob and Tom were unable to locate the mine from the map even with the changes because the map had no explicit placement in the topography of the area.

THE ORTIZ MAP

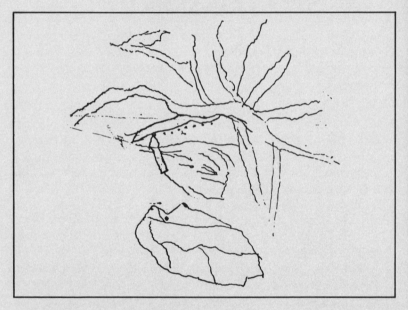

In 1988 Corbin received a phone call from a woman in Northern Arizona. She said she had heard that he was interested in the Lost Dutchman's Mine. She then explained that she had received documents which had belonged to her husband's family from Mesa. Among the papers was a copy of a letter and a map pertaining to a lost mine and she wondered if the Attorney General would like to have them. Of course, he did. That letter is published on the opposite page. It is dated 1864, addressed to Jacob Walsh and signed by Don Peralta. The name is misspelled but the information is so exact one cannot believe it is not Waltz. Even the casual observer can see it was written by an uncertain hand—almost a scribble, on very unusual paper and that it is very old. The information in that letter makes sense and the man who wrote it was having trouble with his English.

Corbin and Kollenborn believe what might have happened is that the two Jacobs decided to desert the sinking Southern Army and head for Mexico because no one would look for them there. Depending on their route, they may have run into Peralta in the cantina at Arispa, saved his life and gone to his ranch where he encouraged them to join him and go into Arizona to dig up the gold with his peons. If that story is true the letter may be the rights to his mine which Peralta is supposed to have given them in return for their share of the ore.

THE ORTIZ LETTER

March 8

... I have a large land
grant in arizona.
In which I have one of the ritchest gold
mines in the world. but
account of the mexicans I had to
leave the country
Now on my age I dont want to risk
my life on acount of indians. If you
want to try I'll send Frank with you
I give you a plot. all right here it is.
First go to torchis mountain then
south side.
go east ward untill a u I find the
first gorge on.
the south side from the west end
follows which
gorge follow
the gorge untill you find a
crooked trail which will lead
you north wards over a lasty
... south ward east
... needle in to a long canyon
... to a tributary canyon
... from the ...
... the mine ...

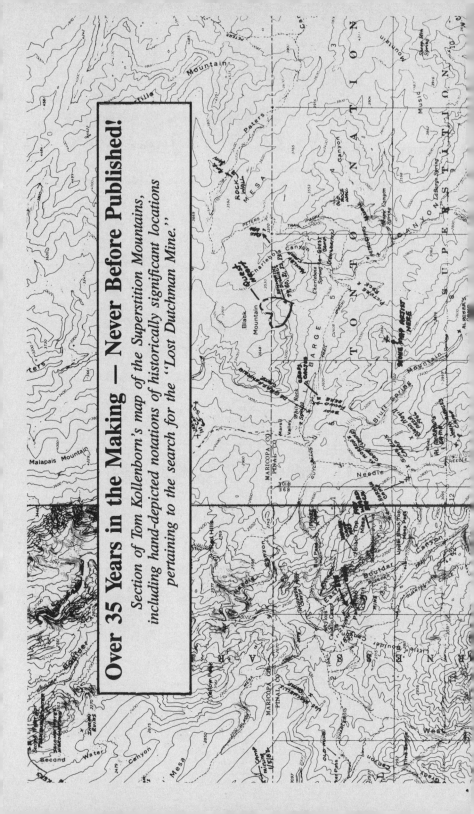

Over 35 Years in the Making — Never Before Published!

Section of Tom Kollenborn's map of the Superstition Mountains, including hand-depicted notations of historically significant locations pertaining to the search for the "Lost Dutchman Mine."

PERALTA LOCATOR MAP

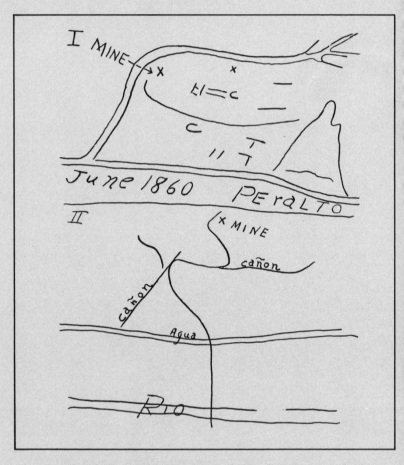

The Peralta locator map is one of the three maps that were received by Erwin Ruth from Senor Gonzales during his trip to Mexico. It is claimed to be one of the maps to the Peraltas' lost gold mines.

THE FISH TREASURE MAP

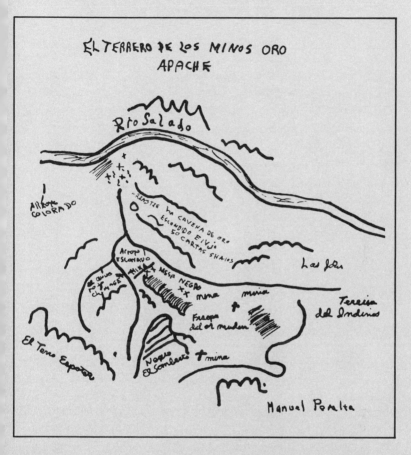

Frank Fish was a successful contemporary treasure hunter. A number of years ago, while searching in Mexico, he met an American mining engineer who told him of a great gold mine in the Superstition Mountains of Arizona. Frank claimed he was eventually able to locate members of the Peralta family who gave him the map. They said the document came from Manuel Peralta. The full story of finding the map appears in a book, "Dead Men Do Tell Tales," by Lake Erie Schafer. The original map is held by the Schafer family.

THE DUTCHMAN'S MAP

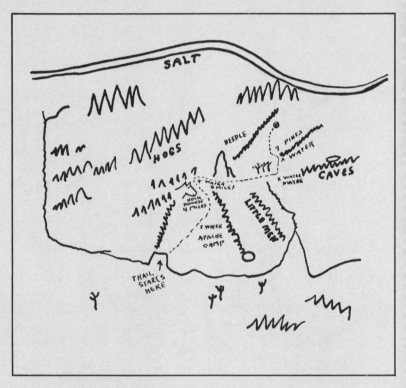

 This particular map is always called the Dutchman's map. Over the years this map and various variations of it has appeared in books and magazines. It is alleged that it is a copy of the many maps which Julia Thomas sold in and around Phoenix to treasure seekers of the Lost Dutchman Gold Mine. She claimed it was a copy of the one that Waltz drew for her just before his death in 1891,

having made the trip in there at least twice before, should run short of grub in so short a time.

Second, I never heard of an Apache Indian leaving a new shirt of any kind hanging on a bush, or leave it on a dead man, or anywhere else if they could get it.

My final deductions in Jacob Walsh's story is that he saw the Apaches crawling up on them and he had a chance to duck and get away, if he did not go to the mine and notify his partner. But he chose to save his own scalp. He probably reasoned that if he went up to the mine to warn his partner they would both lose their lives. It is considered in this country, worse than murder, to desert one's partner in a crisis of that kind, as you are considered a coward as well as a murderer, and that evidently was what Jake Walsh meant when dying when he was asking God to forgive him. Jake Wiser, his partner, could not conceive of such action upon his friend's part and supposed the Apaches had killed him. There must have been a surprise party when they met in the beyond.

Within these pages are some discrepancies which bear examination. After researching the notes of these men I believe a plausible explanation can be offered.

According to all the records, Jim Bark was not the type of man who would have left a story which besmirched anyone. He may not have liked Tom Weedin, but he wasn't going to leave that fact for posterity. Jim was dead by the time Sims wrote his book and, for that matter, so was Tom. Sims was a newsperson and probably felt the story should be told in its entirety.

Another clue to reinforce that hypothesis is the manner in which Jim handled two different matters relating to theft within those notes. When Jim was talking about the gold ore which had disappeared from under Jacob's deathbed, his exact words were, "Helena and Reiney each suspected the other with making away with it, but both were innocent, and it is not necessary to mention the name of the guilty party, so I will pass it."

The other occasion was when Julia and the Petrasch brothers were camped near Jim's ranch and Julia's cloth purse containing

Jacob's papers, the map and sundry mementoes was stolen during the night. Being a gentleman, Jim's quote was, "Who got it, or where it went, I do not wish to say."

Another important matter which needs clarification is Tom Weedin's conversation regarding his and the doctor's search for the Dutchman's mine. Remember, Weedin's wife wouldn't hear of his going into the Superstitions. Perhaps he saw no reason to tell Sims that they would go to search for it in an effort to keep peace at home. There was a code of honor among gentlemen in the Old West and from reading the notes of these two friends I believe it was adhered to strictly. Or, perhaps Weedin wanted to curry favor with the Phoenix newsman regarding his upcoming candidacy. After all, he knew those two men were looking for the mine; everyone knew it. Why didn't he come forth earlier? It appears he wanted Sims' trust. But, whatever the reason, Weedin's account of the plan to mine didn't jibe with Bark's notes.

Of course, Sims was old when he finally wrote the book and his memory probably was fading. There had been reams of information collected. Some of it probably sounded better in one light or another, so he adjusted it.

Who knows? Maybe Walker was a stickler and Weedin didn't want to create any hard feelings. After all, Walker supposedly had said that he didn't want Weedin to talk to anyone about it.

Sims said Walker took $2 million out of the Vekol; Bark said it was $500,000. Given the way gossip exaggerates money and power, there is no doubt that people created whatever impression suited them. Walker was rich; that fact is established in all the books written about him. He was famous and he was considered a blood brother to the Pimas. There is no question that Walker went down in history as an extraordinary pioneer.

All of this matters little in the scheme of things regarding Jacob Waltz. What does matter is that we learned what happened to the other miner. It also seems ironic that both men died of pneumonia. It is sad that they obviously cared about each other but never knew what had happened to the other, until the end

Guard protecting the silver "pigs" in the Wells Fargo office, 1879.

of their days.

There is one word which might have affected Bark's attitude—*Naked.* Sims quoted Julia as having said Jacob found his partner's shirt hanging naked on a shovel handle. Bark said he found his partner's body naked. That could not have been true if Dr. Walker's story is accurate. Why would Tom Weedin lie about a thing like that? Weedin, according to Sims, came in to talk. He had not been close to either Bark or Ely; he could not have known all of the facts regarding that story. When people discuss something that has been researched for a long time they don't recount it all, just the most pertinent facts. I doubt that Weedin knew what Julia had been saying or what Reiney told Bark. It seems likely that Tom Weedin told the story exactly as Dr. Walker expressed it, or as near to it as he could remember.

It is ironic that the matter of Weisner's death should come to light in that manner, and it is an important part of the mystery.

That one factor caused Jim Bark to label Jacob as a murderer and a coward. Unfortunately, for the old man, Jim Bark was considered a paragon of civic responsibility and his word was probably unquestionable. It just doesn't make sense.

If Jacob was greedy enough to kill his partner why did he leave the gold in the cache for so many years? Why didn't he go back and mine as much as he could get? He lived so simply for the rest of his life, it is inconsistent with the rest of the story. And a greedy, selfish murderer would not have pulled Julia out of her debt dilemma. He also would not have tried to give them the mine. He could have sold the rights to that mine for millions of dollars to many willing takers. The big money of Denver, New York and Chicago was already entering the territory and wealthy entrepreneurs were buying up mining claims. That money developed Goldfield, but that is another story to be told in an upcoming book.

Chapter 8

Two Soldiers

The following story is a true reflection of the power of the curse. It involves two young innocents who were murdered. They would take a noted place in the history of Jacob's legend, but they would remain forever nameless.

The incident occurred in the summer of 1884, but it was 1892 before Sims Ely learned of it. At the time the story made little impact on the man and wouldn't become important until it was corroborated by Colonel A. J. Doran in 1910.

There are no documents to prove the story, but we do have Sims' word that it happened and Jim Bark's notes relate an almost identical story. Additionally, Brownie Holmes' notes mention that his father claimed that Jacob Waltz had killed the two soldiers. It is evident that the soldiers did exist and had found rich ore. In Chapter 9 we will discuss the deaths of two other men connected with the soliders. There was an inquest into those deaths. The document reviewing the inquest was found in the papers of the old Silver King Mine. Since it parallels the entire matter so closely, researchers believe the following account.

Bob Bowen, former superintendent of the Silver King Mine, told Sims this story:

It was a summer evening. Two young men appeared in Pinal carrying rolled blankets and light camping equipment. They were

Photograph of the Silver King Mine.

tired. After acquiring lodging, they asked about finding work. They were told the Silver King Mine was about five miles up the road at the foot of the Pinal Mountains, or if they wanted to work at the mill they should see Aaron Mason, the manager of both properties, in the morning.

Colonel Doran was an expert at mill construction. He had supervised the installation of the Pinal Mill where all Silver King ore was reduced. He ran the mill while Bowen ran the mine. As luck would have it, all three men were on hand in Mason's office when the young men arrived.

Immediately, they were questioned regarding their skills. The Silver King was in full swing and good men were always needed. The pair said they had recently been discharged from the Army at Fort McDowell and had decided to stay in the West to seek their fortunes. They seemed to be willing workers and that always interested the superintendent. He introduced them to his

Muckers with dynamite caps.

associates suggesting that they might be muckers for Bowen or work around the mill for Doran.

Muckers gathered the loosened rock after the miners had picked and broken it. It took muscular backs to haul the material in buckets up to the surface where horse-drawn wagons would then take it to the mill to be crushed.

Bowen, noting their apparent strength and honest manner, quickly offered to send them to the mine in a returning ore wagon.

Mason asked if they needed money. Most of the drifters who showed up in his office had spent their last dollar in a gaming hall or were fresh from prospecting where they had come away broke and disillusioned.

Contrary to that fact, the soldiers had saved their Army pay and collectively had about $200 in gold. Although they didn't elaborate, it seemed obvious they were anxious to make as much money as they could. One of them explained they had even declined an offer of government transportation from the fort to Phoenix when they were discharged because it meant taking an expensive stagecoach ride to Florence and then Pinal. The weather was perfect for camping out so they walked.

The mine directors listened politely as the soldiers continued. Their army job had been scouting for renegade Apaches. Of course, that had made them generally familiar with the lay of the land between Fort McDowell and Picket's Post near Pinal.

One of them grimaced at that point, saying they were later sorry they had taken off on foot through such rough terrain. It got so bad in some spots they thought they would have to turn back. At this point something unexpected happened.

The taller of the two said, "In the roughest place we came to we found an old mine." They knew it was a mine because there was a dump and a tunnel. Their years of soldiering had exposed them to a lot of mines ...

200 feet underground — mining gold.

Shift-change at the mine.

They struck out, always trying to work toward their destination, but making very slow progress. They ran on to a trail, and such a queer place for a trail. They concluded to follow it and see if it wouldn't lead them out of that God-forsaken country. They followed it but a short distance and were in hopes when the trail led them through a cave between the peaks. It must have been a foot trail, as animals could not go through the cave. They went on a little further, and came to a tunnel that had been walled up, with working above and over. They said that they did not believe that what they saw was gold, as there was so much of it. They said they certainly could load their burros down to the water line.

Up until this point their conversation had been fairly mundane but Doran would later remember what changed that and why it was indelibly etched in his mind.

"Mr. Mason, that reminds me," one of them said. "I'd like you to look at this stuff and tell us what metal this is? We found it at that mine." Reaching into a sack, he took out some ore.

The mine manager appeared instantly impressed—the ore was

rich with gold. He got up and closed the office door. The executives gathered around the samples as Mason said in an elevated voice, "Why, fellow, this is gold. How much of it have you got?"

A newspaper was quickly spread on the desk and the sack emptied. After careful examination Mason said, "This is hand-sorted ore. And, it's extremely rich. You've got between $600 and $800 worth here. I'll have our assayer retort it for you, and I'll pay full value for this batch. you'll be well fixed for money, I can tell you. But don't waste your time working here. Go back to that old mine and bring away any more of that ore you can find. It's probably an abandoned mine, from what you tell me, and you have the right to take it. How much more of this stuff is laying around?"

The soldiers became excited, both answering at once as the words came tumbling out. "There's lots more there, just like this. Why you could fill a wagon bed with it."

The reader might remember that Jacob Weisner was hard at work when the Apaches attacked. More than likely he was breaking ore at a feverish pace for several days after Waltz left to get supplies. And, perhaps, because he didn't have the help of another strong back, he had let the ore pile up at the site insteading of hauling it to the surface.

"Nonsense!" Mason growled, disbelieving their story. He assured them there couldn't be much more. The manager had been at this game a long time, no one would go off and leave ore that rich lying around in a heap. Then he added confidently, "The Apaches have probably chased the miners away and they haven't thought the mine important enough to come back." He was firm. "It's probably just about worked out."

It was duly noted throughout the territory that gold often was found in pockets and when it was very rich would play out fast. Unfortunately, in those days no one had heard of core-drilling or using metal detectors to find out if nature had sent the vein off in another direction. When old mother nature was belching fissures up through newly formed mountains, she did so at whim.

Fortunately, the young men had stumbled into the office of

an honest man. Mason proceeded to caution them to locate the mine as required by law. Then he questioned their ability to relocate the area where it had been found.

With mounting exuberance the pair said with certainty that they could. One of them explained it was in a northerly direction from a sharp peak which they had seen in their scouting days.

Mason believed they were talking about Weaver's Needle, which in the Spanish days had been called Sombrero Peak.

Soldiering had been a good teacher. Their officers, wanting them to survive, taught them a trick learned from Indian scouts. It was to look back after passing some distinct landmark and make mental notes of unusual rock formations or washes. This they had done. Everyone in that room knew many a man who had become so excited about a find that he would rush off to file a claim, only to realize later that he was hopelessly confused from tracking through similar terrain. In the end he would wind up bitter and frustrated, sometimes spending the rest of his life without relocating the ore.

These two soldiers seemed astute. They went on further explaining how they had struck a trail which led through a little gap in the range not far from the peak. This trail was very old and led them into a valley two miles wide. The valley ran east and west. They had followed the easterly portion until they crossed some canyons. They were certain that was the direction they needed to go—they passed a horse ranch and some corrals. From that ranch the trail led to Pinal.

Concerned for their safety, Mason inquired about guns. Admitting they had purchased pistols at the fort, the pair appeared unconcerned. The mine manager suggested rifles while talking at length about the Apaches. They appreciated the advice and assured him it would be done.

The sincerity which followed attests to Mason's decency. He directed them to locate two lode claims side by side each to be 1,500 feet long by 600 feet wide, with the mine at the center of the track "for elbow room." He offered to make out location notices in duplicate which he told them to place in monuments. His advice included the size and number of monuments. He described the location work which had to be done and counseled them on how to comply with the law. Mason added the latter could wait until after they had recorded duplicate notices at the county seat. "Get two men experienced with powder and drills and you will both need picks and shovels." Sobering, Mason added, "Keep silent about this. Many a good claim has been jumped before all this can be done."

The soldiers asked if they could step outside for a private conversation. When they returned they were intent upon taking Mason in as a partner. He said he would, but thought they were foolish. Pausing for a moment, he finally said he would pay for the exploration and development after they had located the mine.

Mason was reconsidering his earlier impulsiveness. The young soldiers were obviously sincere and seemed particularly eager; perhaps, he too was becoming a believer.

The following day the assayer brought a little over $700 in coin to Mason's office. The soldiers had $200 from their army pay. They decided to leave $300 in gold from their stake with the engineer. Mason promptly put it into a glass jar which was placed in the office safe.

Later, those amounts of money would become a much-discussed clue. Bowen and Doran remembered exactly how much was involved.

Supplies and equipment came to less than $250. Thus, the soldiers left Pinal for the mine with not quite $400 in gold and silver coin on their persons.

The trek started after dark and they were never seen alive again.

After a lengthy discussion everyone had agreed the trip and the work would take no more than 10 days. Two weeks had passed and Mason was defintely uneasy. Fearing the Apaches had taken them, Mason sent out 20 seasoned men to search within the region of Weaver's Needle. The party split into small groups always within hearing of a warning rifle shot. They failed to locate the pair, and, what was unusual, they failed to locate any of their equipment.

At this point we will make a slight departure from Sims' story to add some pertinent information supplied by Jim Bark.

Quoted Bark, "My authority for this was Wiley Homan, who sometimes lived at Pinal, following mining and then he would change and go to cow punching. He was considered as truthful as a combined miner and cow puncher could be. Wiley told me that he had seen the gold and had discussed it with Mason on different occasions. Years later Wiley wrote to Mrs. Mason in New York in regard to the gold, and she replied that she had such a jar with two names on it; that a mining friend had told her there was about three hundred dollars worth of gold in the jar, and that it was subject to the owner's claim."

Bark also described in detail where the soldiers had gone. And, since some of our readers may want to search for the mine or track these two men on Tom's map, I will enclose their exact words as Wiley told it.

They struck out towards the King, crossed Salt River, and struck a trail which they had been told was the proper one to take, and which is now called the Apache Trail, but it is now an automobile road. They followed it for several miles to a creek crossing, where there was water. The trail after that appeared to run nearly north, and the King was nearly south, so while they felt certain that the trail would eventually land them at the King it must be a long way around and they were tired. They decided to make a short cut, went up this creek for some distance, came to a waterfall and could go no further. They came back down the creek, and finally got out on the side of the creek toward the King, and up on a very high mountain. There was no trail.

Jim Bark's notes included some more information.

The hat found beside the body was sent to the Sutler's store at Fort McDowell. The store owner said it had been purchased by one of the discharged soldiers who started afoot for the Silver King Mine on a certain date, giving his name, which was correct.

He had a bullet hole in his back and had been dead long enough so that the body was pretty well decomposed. Old man Whitlow, who was one of the men who found the body, said that there had been a shod horse track on the trail leading over the mountain into the Superstitions. He said they just dug a shallow hole, rolled the body into it, covered him with what little dirt they had, piled rocks on the grave to keep the animals from digging him up and let it go at that. Bark said:

> This grave was shown to me by one of the Whitlow boys. It was about a quarter of a mile above my ranch house. Huse Ward and I dug him up, and found nothing but bones and buttons, so we reburied him and recovered the grave. It is still there undisturbed. Bill Kimball of Mesa, said that at about that time he saw the body of a man (Naked) lying near Bluff spring, so he pulled out for Mesa immediately. Whether this was the other soldier is only conjecture, but I am inclined to think that it was, as there were very few white men traveling in the Superstitions at the time. One thing certain, neither of the Soldiers was ever seen afterward.

Note: Indians never rode shod horses. Now back to Sims' story:

> The mine manager, upon learning of the search results, decided he might have been wrong about the locale. Maybe it was Tortilla Mountain, which is 6 miles northeast of Weaver's Needle. It was even larger than the Needle from some directions.
> By accident he ran into Will Whitlow, a cattleman from Queen Creek. Asking if Will knew the Needle Country, Mason became hopeful. Whitlow knew it well and offered to go with one of his hands to search.
> The distance from the Whitlow Ranch to Bark Ranch is less than 15 miles. On that trail Will found a partially decomposed nude body which had a bullet hole in it. Nearby they found a hat—their only clue to the man's identity. The two cowboys dug a crude grave and buried the body. Later, Mason sadly identified the hat as having belonged to one of the soldiers.
> Apaches usually stripped their victims before torture; then they would steal whatever was useful, especially stock. Horses were kept for use in their travels and burros were used as food.
> This particular saga took many turns, raising more intrigue in the legend and proving there was a curse on the gold.

Before long, doubt about the murder began to grow in Pinal. By now the story was buzzing through saloons, stores, the mine and the mill.

Generally, in the saloons of mining camps, elderly men performed cleaning and repair jobs. In Pinal, however, the swamper was a husky young man who, unfortunately, had been born with a twisted foot. Mining, mucking and timbering jobs were only for the hearty with two good arms and legs. Rather than being an object of any sympathy, this particular fellow's irritating manner had evoked ire from the locals.

A chronic cadger who wheeled coins and chips at the faro tables after a constant vigilance with a lucky player, the swamper would then gamble, much to the dealers' disgust. The moocher had a definite taste for gambling without any means to support it.

A week after the soldiers left, the swamper began gambling with gold and silver coins. To explain his newfound wealth he claimed he had been in a game on a trip to Florence. It was just a lucky streak. For the moment the locals accepted the story.

Later, when the news reached Pinal and the Silver King that Whitlow had found a body thought to be one of the soldiers, a saloonkeeper jokingly said to the swamper, "Say, you've been out of camp. Did you do that killing?" Both men laughed. A customer standing nearby overheard the remark. He had seen the moocher gambling with gold coin; so started a new theory. The swamper wasn't well liked anyway but a strong sense of justice prevailed in the camps. True, it was frontier justice, but justice nonetheless. Mason was well respected and probably had spoken highly of the soldiers.

A local who happened to be going to Florence was commissioned to make inquiries. The man was thorough. The swamper had not been seen in Florence and further, all freighters and stage drivers were questioned. None of them could remember him having ridden with them. And, because of his lowly station, he did not own a horse.

It had been assumed, and later ascertained, that both boys had been killed. The body of the other soldier was later found in a thicket just off the trail a mile away from his partner. Both men had been shot.

Maricopa Wells stage station, Pinal, Arizona.

Arizona miners meet the stagecoach.

HELEN CORBIN

Everyone's suspicions were raised, but wishing to be fair, inquiries were made within a broad radius as to a possible burglary or holdup at some wayside site or stage-station. Still, nothing of that sort was reported, and the swamper had been missing right after the soldiers left.

By now residents remembered the boys purchasing equipment which they had said was for prospecting. They had been seen by many people paying their bills with gold coin from a sack. And, it was well-known that more than one holdup or murder committed by Mexicans or whites had been blamed on the savages by simply imitating the Indians' normal rituals.

The swamper was questioned and the results left locals even more suspicious. Rumors abounded about Frontier Justice. Tempers flared with repeated questioning; the swamper grew sullen and silent.

The inquisitors gathered in the saloon's poker room. Bob Bowen was in camp from the mine; he was requested to join the discussion. They then reconstructed the crime detail by detail arriving at the conclusion that the swamper was the murderer. There were some who were all for hangin' the fellow. Bob Bowen became angry, "Arizona is law-abiding territory," he raged back. "We don't lynch men out here."

Someone suggested they give the swamper a few hours to get out of camp once and for all time.

"That's right," Bowen said. "I'm for that. We will know he's a no-good loafer. Let's get rid of him."

The swamper was way ahead of them. At that moment he was on a stagecoach halfway to Florence. He was never seen in Arizona again.

The irony of life is sometimes almost unbelievable. Because of Ely's and Bark's diligence, little-known facts surfaced and were recorded. Fortunately, their running account of the saga now makes a case almost as valid as one kept by Scotland Yard or a file in a good investigator's office. Like Tom Kollenborn, they were hungrier for truth than for gold.

Mason was probably the only one who knew the soldiers' names. He was alone with them the day they put the gold into

137

the safe. Colonel Doran believed he remembered Mason telling him that after the tragedy the latter had forwarded the $300 he had in the office safe to the soldiers' parents. But it was many years later before the Colonel imparted that story to Sims Ely and, by this time, believe it or not, Mason had been killed by the curse. That story will be told later in Chapter 11.

It hadn't occurred to any of the men involved to record the soldiers' names, and at this particular juncture Sims had not yet decided to write his book. To this day all three men are without identity.

A further bit of evidence came about in 1915—some five years after Colonel Doran corroborated the story which Sims had heard by chance in 1892.

For some unknown reason Sims was handling the affairs of a bank which had failed in Phoenix. An aide told Sims he had a visitor named Pankinin. Assuming the caller was there on bank business, Sims invited him in.

After entering, the man said he was Earnest Albert Pankinin, recently from Alaska. Continuing, Albert described his birthplace and whereabouts all of his life, saying that tuberculosis had originally brought him to Arizona. He further stated that upon recovery he had gone to Alaska, become ill again and was now back in the sunshine for good.

Sims must have looked puzzled. Pankinin explained that he hoped his honesty would garner Sims' trust.

Of course, the newsman's interested piqued, but he was cautious, watching his visitor carefully. The man's face appeared deeply lined and he looked tired about the eyes. His illness could have been the cause. Sims noted, however, that he had a well-shaped head, very honest gray eyes and an expressive, pleasant mouth.

They were to know each other for a long time to come and Sims never had any reason to alter his good opinion of the man.

"In Alaska," Mr. Pankinin said, "I was told some things about the Superstition Mountains that I regard as immensely important. That's the real reason I came to Phoenix instead of going to Yuma. I want to find out something about those mountains. I've been told that you and Jim Bark have been looking for an old mine in those hills and that you two know more about them than anyone else. I'm also interested in finding an old mine." He said he knew Jim Bark had a ranch up in those mountains but was never able to make contact with the man. Then, he said if Sims didn't want to share information he would understand because he had information which also would have to remain a secret.

Surprised, the newsman spoke candidly, which probably pleased Pankinin. Sims openly admitted that he and Bark had searched for such a mine for a long time. "In fact," he said with aplomb, "there's not much Jim and I are keeping to ourselves, except our conclusions about the map we have. So I'll be able to tell you anything I can. If, later on, you should ask me something I didn't care to give out, I'd just tell you so."

Mr. Pankinin, obviously relieved, asked, "Do you know anything about a Green Spring situated four or five miles to the west of the old Silver King Mine?"

The Silver King had played out by that time and Pinal was a ghost town. Sims recalled going out there with friends for a drive. He nodded and smiled. "Yes," he said, "It was covered with a greenish scum and is about the distance you mentioned."

The visitor's eyes sparkled and he was quick to say that was the information he had been desperately seeking. He was already extracting a notebook from an inside coat pocket. When it was opened he exposed a sheet showing lines drawn from the words "Phoenix, Florence, Silver King and Green Spring." The ink line ran northeast to the Silver King, then west to the Green Spring—the last line extended westerly without pointing out any destination.

Pankinin's excitement mounted as he explained his search for the past weeks, then he added, "You're the first one I've found who knew of it. Have you ever been there?"

Sims said he had stopped there for lunch with friends on a weekend trip to the old ghost town.

That spring, Pankinin said, was the key on the route to the old mine. Then, becoming cautious again, he explained the rest of his map was on another piece of paper helped out by secret details he kept to himself. He seemed confident that upon arrival at that point on the map he would recognize the topography and be able to find the mine. "The whole thing was given to me by a friend in Alaska and I believe he told the truth. And, now, I'll tell you why."

One can just imagine that Sims was inwardly sympathetic but amused. How many times had he heard these words? To this day we hear it over and over again. Given the clues why not—it sounds so simple until the optimist actually goes into those indomitable twisted canyons still clutching their treasure with iron hands.

Pankinin told his story. The tale seemed fairly ordinary with one bizarre exception.

In Alaska the man had been employed doing clerical work during the winters. Summers he tried his luck at prospecting but with few rewards. His health held and he continued to hope.

Pankinin's work involved traveling and eventually, after moving to a position of authority, he settled in a town.

A fellow employee, who he called Robertson (and which was obviously not a true name), had a problem. Pankinin solved the dilemma for the laborer causing him to be indebted. It seems the man had physical problems; Pankinin found him lighter work at better wages and the employee was thoroughly grateful. Later, Robertson became ill and Pankinin visited him frequently; their friendship strengthened.

On one visit they discussed Pankinin's intention to return to the states permanently. The question naturally came up as to where Pankinin would settle.

Of course, ill health would bring the man back. He stated as much, saying Arizona had just the right climate for his condition.

Robertson's interest piqued as he said that he ardently wished he could go also. Then, the man offered some information which he said would make a fortune for Pankinin.

Pankinin became interested.

"It's a gold mine—the richest mine ever found anywhere, I do believe," Robertson said.

Pankinin was instantly deflated, stating, "A lot of good that will do me."

Robertson insisted it was a forgotten mine and assured his friend if it hadn't been he would have heard about it, "even up here."

Instantly, Pankinin's enthusiasm raised. He encouraged Robertson to come along stating that he could afford the trip.

The man's refusal was quick and firm in a tone of voice which defied further argument. Pankinin wasn't stupid, he made his own assumptions as to why a man wouldn't go back to such a treasure.

The sick man seemed suddenly uneasy, Albert noted, but he drew a map directing that it be cut into two pieces and instructing the final details be committed to memory.

By this time Sims Ely was properly fascinated. He asked, "How old is your friend now?"

Pausing, Pankinin searched for an answer. "Around seventy, I'd say."

Wrinkling a brow, Sims replied, "That's pretty well up in years for a man to be working in Alaska, especially with a physical defect."

"Yes," Pankinin said, "He's very slow now, he has a twisted foot."

For the next seven years Pankinin worked as a guard at the Phoenix National Bank, still searching in vain.

Whenever the pair chanced to meet, Pankinin would rush to tell Sims why he had not been able to locate the mine. He had even tried to renew contact with Robertson—only to learn the former swamper from Pinal had died.

In the meantime Sims was never able to convince Jim Bark to allow Pankinin to become a partner in their quest.

Albert Pankinin, like all the others, was confident until the end that one day he would find the Lost Dutchman. He therefore never revealed any of the special knowledge of the final clues. He died on December 21, 1934 and the secret died with him.

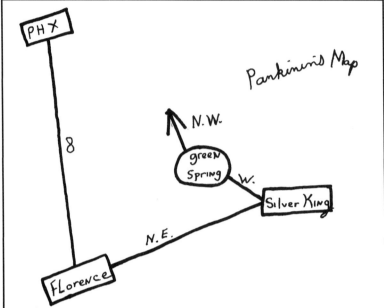

The story of the mysterious Mr. Pankinin appears in Chapter 8 of this book. He claims to have received it from a sick friend in Alaska. He never found the mine and readily admitted that it was not at all on the paper; much of it was committed to memory. He was also looking for a spring which seems to have dried up after the big earthquake in the late 1800s.

Chapter 9

Deering and Chuning—
Gold Fever Deaths

The fate of the two soldiers became an oft discussed mystery among the people of the Silver King Mine. Of course, Pankinin's appearance on the scene and his involvement with Sims Ely explained the disappearance of the swamper at the Silver King Saloon. It seems likely that he followed and killed the two soldiers—how else could he have known of the mine's location? There also was the fact that he had enough money to get to Alaska. Why did he run so far so fast if there was nothing to fear?

We now know that Pankinin's last days were spent searching for the elusive treasure to no avail.

The list continues.

The next name to come to light in the quest for the Dutchman's mine was Joe Deering (also spelled Dearing). When he died there was an inquest held in Pinal County and presided over by Judge R. J. Whiteside, acting coroner. According to inquest documents found in archival records of the Silver King Mine the inquest was held on September 27, 1885 and filed October 23, 1885 by a county clerk named W. R. Stone. The inquest documents are included at the end of this chapter to verify that Joe Deering did exist.

It seems expedient to include in this chapter the references made to Joe Deering and his friend, John Chuning, in both Jim Bark's notes and those of Brownie Holmes. One might also note that both men told a similar story.

From Bark's notes:

In the summer of 1885 Joe Deering, looking for work, rode into the Silver King's freight corrals. After learning that jobs were available he refused an offer to sell his horse. He was later quoted as having said, "I'll need it by and by."

Everyone who came to know Deering said that he was a dedicated man with an eagerness to keep busy. This fact surfaced almost immediately. Bowen, who hired him, explained that they would shut the Silver King down temporarily to retimber the main shaft below.

Undaunted, Deering went to one of the saloons. The keeper, Daniel Brown, happened to be on hand as the miner entered. "You got anything around here I can do?" Deering asked. "It's not that I'm broke, I just like to keep busy."

Brown said later he liked the young man and, after making certain he didn't drink or gamble, gave him a job.

As time went on Brown learned quite a bit about Deering. As they worked, Deering confided the story of prospecting California, Colorado and Arizona. He said his partner's name was Thompson. The pair had been working around Prescott for the past year but without much luck. Deering was waiting for Thompson to arrive.

Brown and Deering became fast friends, but it was only after Brown admitted he had no absolutely no interest in mines or gold. He loved the saloon business and intended to stay in it. It was quite evident he liked Joe Deering and was keenly interested in the colorful stories which Joe conveyed about himself, his partner and their travels.

Later, in a moment of confidence, Deering told Brown he had found a gold mine in Arizona and as soon as Thompson arrived, the pair would lay claim to it. He then explained why he had come to the area. He said, after hearing about the soldiers, he figured the Apaches had killed them. Using astute powers of deduction, Deering eventually discovered the site and described the place as ghostly.

Sims Ely relocated Brown some 20 years later. The saloon-keeper had long since retired to the town of Florence. He said Brown was along in years, but his mind was as clear as a bell and he was graphic in his description of the event.

Brown explained that Deering described the following: "The mine was a kind of pit, shaped like a funnel; the large opening at the top. The pit was partly filled in with debris." Deering figured it had been washed in by heavy rains. "There was a considerable quantity of this rich ore on the surface." He said that on the hillside below the pit was a portal to a tunnel. It had been walled up with rocks, but one or two of them had fallen from the top layer, and through the opening Deering could see the tunnel pointed toward the pit. It was that tunnel they were going to investigate when his partner arrived.

Later, Joe got his job at the Silver King and soon became friendly with John Chuning, his shift boss. While they were eating from their lunchpails one night, Deering showed John a sample of rich ore.

Naturally, Chuning asked a lot of questions. Deering was evasive, and he never admitted it had come from the mine discovered by the two soldiers. He did volunteer one statement which later puzzled everyone who heard the story. Chuning quoted him as saying, "John, there's a trick to the trail. Oh, not much of a trick—but you have to go through a hole." No one could ever decide whether he meant a crevice or an actual hole in the rock.

Within a week after he had begun to work in the Silver King, James Green, Thomas Gormley and Joe Deering were timbering down in the bowels of the Silver King. A small piece of rock hit Deering's neck as he stood high on a plank. He leaped to the ground. At the same time a scale of rock slipped from the face of the shaft hitting his leg. Joe's cries echoed in the tunnel. Green jumped off the staging and caught him under the arms all the while calling for help. Six or seven miners rushed in and lifted Deering up. Joe was begging for water and crying that his leg was broken.

White.· PINAL COUNTY Record
OCT 2, 1885 P. 3 col 2

On last Saturday night, at the King mine, Joseph Deering met with a terrible accident which terminated in his death Sunday morning. It appears while he was working in the 500 foot level a large boulder rolled over him literally mashing a portion of his body almost to pulp. He was immediately conveyed to his room, and Dr. Kenniard called in to attend him. Amputation was necessary, but he was so weak from the loss of blood, that he died while the physician was in the act of taking off his leg. No blame is attached to the company. Coroner's inquest rendered a verdict of accidental death. The company suspended work and attended the funeral. Mr. Deering was a good man and well liked by his friends and fellow-workmen.

News copy dated Oct. 2, 1885 verifies Deering's death.

Carrying Joe to the station, the team put him into the cage which went clanking to the surface. The men watched in silence as the iron carrier rose out of sight. Gormley said later, the rock which crushed Deering's leg probably weighed 500 or 600 pounds. And it had not just broken the bones, it had crushed the leg.

The doctor at the mine testified that there was much blood and damage to the leg above the knee. He gave the tortured man morphine and applied a tourniquet. A crew removed Deering to his cabin. By seven that evening it was evident the miner's leg would have to be amputated, and by one o'clock the next afternoon, Joe Deering, the man who had found Jacob's mine, was dead. The curse had claimed another victim.

Bark's Notes on Joe Dearing

One day in the late 80's there came to the ranch a man and camped down at the well. He had a burro and a pup. That evening he came up to the house, and we were talking on general subjects, when he said that the King had shut down, and that he did not want to go to town. He was speaking of the Silver King mine which was about fifteen miles southeasterly from us. It had produced between fourteen and fifteen million dollars in silver, but now had shut down for an indefinite time. He thought he would rest up for a while.

I asked him to stop with me at the ranch and his grub would cost him nothing. I was busy cleaning water holes. The next morning I was pumping water and letting it run down a pipe about five hundred feet to a string of troughs for cattle. We had been without rain for quite a while and water was getting low in the well and all of the water holes.

This man, whose name was John Chuning, suggested that we sink or drift from the bottom of the well and under the creek, after pumping it dry and making an examination, and that he would do the work gladly and not charge anything. So he pumped and kept the water down and I made an examination, and we concluded to drift. What time I could spare away from the other half dozen water holes on various parts of the range, I put in helping John. I think he was one of the most efficient men I ever saw and one of the hardest workers, as well as one of the most truthful.

Well, he drifted in the well and about doubled the flow of water. One evening after supper, I said, "John, what will you work for per day until you get all the water holes fixed up in good shape, those that have to be kept clean from this ranch?" He thought a moment, and said, "Two dollars a day and board." I hired him and told him that he would frequently have to do his own cooking, which he said was all right.

He fixed all the water holes and then built a rock granary, the walls of which are in perfect shape today. One evening, John

The following excerpts are from the Coroner's inquest held at the Silver King Mine in 1885 regarding the accidental death of Joe Deering. These quotes are taken out of context.

JUSTICE COURT SILVER KING
PRECINT PINAL COUNTY ARIZONA
BEFORE R. J. WHITESIDE JUDGE
ACTING AS CORONER.

IN THE MATTER OF THE
INQUESTITION UPON the
remains of Joseph
DEERING DESEASED

Record and

September 27. A.D. 1885

Filed October 23, 1885
W. R. Stone
CLERK

IN THE JUSTIC court, Silver King
Precient Pinal COUNTY, ARIZONA
September 27. A.D. 1895
BEFORE B. J. Whiteside - J.P.
ACTING AS CORONER

IN THE MATTER OF THE
INQUISITION upon the
remains of
Joseph Deering DESEASED,

JURY SUMMONED

W. C. TRUMAN, T.E. THOMPSON, Joseph
McCount. THOMAS ASHTON, P. STILLMAN.
KENNETH MACKENZIE, R.D. DERAIN
F.E. BENTON, J.B. McNEID

JURY SWORN

W. C. TRUMAN, T.E. THOMPSON, JOSEPH
McCount, THOMAS ASHTON, P. STILLMAN
KENNETH MACKENZIE AND J.B. McNEID.

REMAINS OF THE DECEASED VIEWED AND
EXAMINED

JURY ACCOMPANIED by ACTING CORONER
VISITED THE PLACE IN THE SILVER KING

Q. what is your name, occupation and
Residence
A. JAMES XRGEN. MINER, SILVER KING
ARIZONA
Q DID YOU KNOW JOE DEERING IN
HIS LIFE TIME,
A. YES SIR; ABOUT 2 YEARS.
Q. WHEN DID YOU LAST SEE HIM ALIVE
A. THIS MORNING AT 5 o'cloct

149

Q. PLEASE STATE THE CIRCUMSTANCES attending The accident that Befell him last night

A. About 2 o'clock this morning, I september 27, 1885, the deceased, THOMAS GORMLEY, AND myself, were working Together on the second Floor of the 600 Foot wall of the Silver king mine in this County And territory, We were Timbering, a scale of rock fell out, HE WAS STANDING ON A plank when a small piece of rock struck him in the back, and as he looked around the scale of Rock from the side FELL AND STRUCK HIM. IT Fell very quickly, He made a jump from off the plank where he was STANDING from us;

OF THE ROCK. IT caught him and he hollered and said his leg was broken. I Jumped off the STAGING and caught him under the ARMS, AND hollered for help. Six or 7 men came instantly and raised the rock and lifted him up, He Asked FOR A DRINK OF WATER and TO TAKE HIM OUT TO THE STATION Quick, we took him TO The STATION AND GOT HIM ON THE CAGE and SENT him to The surface, I returned to my work.

Q. How much do you think That rock weighed

A. AS A rough estimation I SHOULD JUDGE between 500 AND 600 pounds.

Q 'Did that rock appear to you to be
dangerous before it fell:
D: It did not.
Q Did he seam to bleed freely from
the wond as you took him to the
Station
A. Yes

/9
He was ither removed to His cabin,
a little whiskey and water given him.
I think after he was romoved to His
cabin he had another dose of
morphine. But am not certain,
Nor as to the Time. at about 7
o'cluct I ampultated above the knee.
After that stimulon was freely
used. Hyperdermically. That was
all of the Treatement. He died almost
half pass one o'clock,
Q. What was the immidiate cause of
his death, Nervous Shock or loss
of blood.
A Loss of blood
                    Thomas H. kinnaird M.D.

I hereby certfry that the Above and
Forgoing testimony was carefully
read over to whitness's Thomas H.
Kinnaird. before he sighed Same
                    D J. whiteside JP
                    acting as coroner

said, "Well, Mr. Bark, the granary is about finished and I don't suppose you have any more work for me."

I settled up with John and gave him an order on Goldman's store, at Phoenix, as at that time they were our bankers. John handed the order back to me, and said as I was going to Phoenix for supplies the next day, John would make out a list of grub, and for me to have it sent up with my supplies, and the leave the balance of the order to his credit in Goldman's.

That evening, we were sitting outside the house when he said, "Mr. Bark, do you know that there is a rich gold mine over the mountain?" Then he launched forth as follows: that while he was working at the Silver King, a fellow by the name of Joe Deering asked for work. The foreman, who was Bob Bowen, asked if he was a miner, and he said that he was; so he was told that he could go on at the next shift, and to report to John Chuning, who was a shift boss in the Silver King.

This Deering had one poor ratty burro and a very small and disreputable camping outfit. He had been working but a short time when he spoke to John and said, "I am only going to work here about thirty days." John did not reply as that was a common occurrence, and in a little while he said, "I got a rich gold mine over in the Superstition mountains, and it is some mine." John said, "If you got a rich mine over there, you don't need to work here at all, as you can get a partner and he will put up the money and work it." Deering replied that he did not want a partner, as he had one, and that was the cause of his working now. He said that a merchant up in Colorado had staked him to prospect about eleven months ago, and the law of Colorado says that anything found by a man within one year after accepting a prospecting stake, one-half of such find shall belong to the man who furnished the stake, and as the year has about thirty days to run here, he will work here until the time expires and locate the mine.

John said, "Supposing some one should locate the mine while you are working here?" "Oh, there is no danger of anyone's finding it." John said, "You found it, why couldn't some one else do the same?" "There is no danger, as the mine is in the most ungodly place you ever saw or heard of." During all this conversation, they were working away, side by side. John said that Deering kept referring to his find, and said that if anyone should find the mine, that he had put up a little monument within a hundred feet of it, but that one could not see the mine from the monument and he did not put any notice on it. John asked why. He replied that if anyone should find it he could swear that his monument was there ahead of him, and that he had destroyed the location notice.

John said, "How did you come to find it?" "Well, I was camped at a spring in a big canyon and was headed for the King. I had my breakfast, took my canteen full of water and went to look for my burro. I saw him about half way up the side of the mountain and about a mile and a half up the canyon and above the camp. As I started up toward him, I saw a deep worn trail and it was so much larger and worn so much deeper in the rocks than any trail I had seen on those mountains that it excited my curiosity. I left the burro and started to follow it and believe I followed it six or seven miles and came to the worst place I ever saw. There was a tunnel and it had been walled up."

John said it probably had caved in. Deering said, "No, I am enough of a miner to tell when a tunnel has been walled up. The wall had settled about eight inches, and I don't know how deep the tunnel was. Above the tunnel, and further over, it looked as though there had been two big shafts, but they were pretty well filled."

He returned to his camp, over the same trail which he took going in. On his way back, there was a willow tree growing just at the lower edge of the trail. He rested under it and took the little hand ax he was carrying and cut a cross in the tree." (I found the willow tree and sure enough, the cross was there.) There was an old hatchet picked up on the same trail by a man by the name of Wright. The head of the hatchet was all battered out of shape from pounding rock, and the trail as monumented with two little rocks, until it left Havalina Canyon and dropped over into the horse country.

Dearing said that he would not have stayed all night alone at the mine for all the money in the world. John asked him why not. He said it was so ghostly and creepy. I cannot understand how a man like Deering, who had come all the way through the mountains from Colorado, alone every night, with not even a dog, could gather such fear from this particular spot. The next morning, after thinking it over, he concluded that he would visit the mine once more, so he went over the same trail, but in going back to his camp from the mine, he said that he came down off the big mountain into a canyon and there he built four monuments. He said they were not much monuments—just a long slim stone stood on end with four or five small stones laid around its base, with no particular attention paid to distances or directions.

"What in the world was your idea of doing that?" John asked him. He replied, "I thought if anyone saw the monument at the mine and then saw these, they would think that crazy prospector has been here also, or if they saw these first, and then the one I built at the mine, they would say the same thing and pay no attention to either." (Now I have found the monuments, without a doubt, that Deering built in the canyon.)

Deering said then that he went up the canyon to his camp, and the next day came over to the King. John asked him how far it was from the Salt River. The reply was, "Oh, a mile, mile and a half, two miles."

John said that Deering could not help talking about it, and would keep breaking forth, saying, "John, there is a trick on that trail. Oh, it is no trick either, but you have to go through a cave or hole, and say, John, it is high up and yet you got to go down to it. Say, John, when I work that mine, I am going out the other way, toward the desert. Oh, you don't think I have a mine—you think I am just stringing you, just to be talking. You meet me at Jesse Brown's saloon tonight, and I will show you some of the ore that I picked up in front of the tunnel and evidently was thrown away as waste. If it was, you can judge what the ore they packed out must have been."

Jesse Brown kept a saloon in Pinal, where the mill for the Silver King was located, and the only time Jesse could get away was when Chuning would come down and tend bar for him, which he frequently did when off shift. So Deering showed up that evening and he showed John and Jesse Brown about five pounds of gold ore, and John said it was quite rich. The gold in the different pieces was from split peas to coffee kernels in size.

While I did not in the least doubt John's story, I went on a hunt for Jesse Brown and finally located him in Nogales, Arizona. Upon interviewing him, he verified what John had told me.

A few days after that, Deering was working in a stope in the King, when a cave-in took place and he was quite badly hurt. A fellow workman, Ed Jones of Mesa, put a box on the elevator, sat upon it and held Deering in his lap to the top. He was put upon the operating table, examined, and it was found that he had both legs broken, besides other injuries. The legs were so badly injured that the company doctor decided that amputation was necessary. Deering never recovered consciousness.

I went to the county seat and found the record of where they had held an inquest on one Joe Deering. The verdict was accidental death, and that proved that part of the story.

John said, "I will go over and make a hunt for the mine, for a while at least." I told John that I would be pleased if he would make the ranch his headquarters, and any time he needed any grub to come to the ranch and get it, or any time that he wanted anything from town, I would see that it would be sent out to the ranch. John thanked me, and said under those conditions he ought to find it.

He came over to the ranch about once a month with his burros and his little cur dog. I remember one August night, we were sitting out in front of the house. The moon was shining full and it was hot. John was sitting on our rodeo table which was leaning against the front of the house. John had his shoes and stockings off, as his feet were swollen from climbing. I was sitting on a chair further out from the house to get more breeze. John started to get off the table when his little dog rushed from under the table and took hold of one of John's bare feet.

He said, "What ails that dog?" and settled in his seat on the table again. The dog quieted down, and in a few minutes John made a more determined effort to get down. The dog went through the same performance of taking hold of John's foot, and when he saw that John meant to step down, he let go of his foot and rushed at a rattler coiled right under John's feet. The dog killed the rattler, but was bitten on the nose and the side of the head. There was some water down in the creek, and the dog went down, buried himself all but the tip of his nose in the mud and water, and in the morning was still there. His head was the size of three heads. He stayed there for three days and came up to the house as sorry a looking dog as one ever saw. He never amounted to much after that. All he wanted to do was lie around in the shade. Unless John kept calling him, he would not go over the mountains with him.

Well, John hunted for about a year and went broke and wanted to quit. But I would not hear of it and told him that he had hunted so long, that this was no time to quit as he must have covered a whole lot of country, and that we would stay with it until we ran down. John loaded up and went back over the mountains. The dog followed a Mexican freighter, who had just delivered a load at the ranch and we saw him no more.

John continued to hunt, and at times he would have to take a layoff at the cow ranch and keep off his feet as much as possible as both his knee joints would swell to double their normal size.

John had told me that he had worked for Johnny Ayres, who had a horse ranch up near the Grand Canyon. He had been developing water for Ayres. One time when John was at the ranch, I returned from Phoenix, and the first thing John would grab would be the Arizona Republican. In it, he read of Johnny Ayres' committing suicide. "Well," John remarked, "I must just as well tear this note up. Poor Johnny." John had gone into the house where he kept his go-away bag and dug a paper from within. I asked him what it was that he was going to tear up. He replied that when he got through working for Johnny he took a note for his pay as Johnny had no money. The note was for four hundred and some dollars. I remarked, "Don't tear it up, John. Let me have it, and I will see what I can do with it the first time I go to Phoenix."

I made a few inquiries in Phoenix, and someone told me that E. J. Bennett was a silent partner of Johnny. So I took a chance, went to E. J. Bennett's office, told him that Chuning was hunting for a lost mine up in the Superstition mountains, and was worse than broke; that he was getting along in years, as he was over sixty; that he had a note of Johnny Ayres for work he had done on the horse ranch, etc. E. J. said, "Have you the note with you?" and I produced it. He looked it over, took a pencil and figures the interest, reached for his check book and asked me who he should make the check to. I said, "To me." He made it to me and it called for six hundred and some dollars. When I handed John the certificate of deposit, he thanked me. From then on he would not take a dollar from me. He continued to hunt for the mine, and still made the ranch his headquarters. He built numerous rope ladders to let himself down over cliffs in which could be seen caves, and which were absolutely unapproachable in any other way. Rope ladders that I would not trust myself upon, he would go down twenty-five and thirty feet, and if anything gave way it was "Katey bar the door for John."

He also ran a tunnel one hundred and fifty feet, along a crack in a hill near the Paint mine, north of Sombrero Butte. The crack was about eighteen inches wide and filled with boulders. He ran the entire distance without any timbering, and all alone. Every foot had to be blasted, with no possibility of their being a mine or any ore. I think it was the most dangerous piece of work I ever saw accomplished by man.

Whenever John ran out of money, he would quit hunting and go to work generally for Bill Kimball, who kept a hotel and livery stable in Mesa. John would take care of the livery part of it, and he was a number one worker. Kimball told me that he was always glad to get him.

One day coming from town, I found John resting at the ranch. He showed me a piece of ore and I could see a little free gold in it. I asked him where he got it and he said over in the box canyon of Salt River, above where Fish Creek comes in. He asked me if I thought it was very good. I told him the ore was good enough; it depended upon the quantity. I asked him if he found it in place, and he said he did. I also asked him how wide and long it was, and he said he did not know, but that he did not think much of it. I asked him if he could show it to me, and he said he could and would go any time I was ready.

157

The next day we took a pack horse and two saddle horses and rode to within about two miles of the vein, but that two miles was a holy terror to get over, even on foot, but we got there with most of our clothing torn off and many skinned places. After examination of the vein, I told John that we might run into something pretty good by tunneling, and I thought that we had better spend a little money on it. He said, "All-right," that the money spent on it would not have much of a we to it, as he was in his usual condition financially broke, but that he was willing to work on it.

So I located it in his and my name and then told him that the first thing was a trail. We went back to the cow ranch, packed John's burros with grub and tools, and established camp on the river about two miles from the prospect. We had powder, picks and shovels and finally finished our trail. Some of it, to put it mildly, was very dangerous, as it was built along a cliff about five hundred feet above the river, and fifteen hundred feet above us to the top of the cliff. The fifteen hundred feet above us did not concern us much as there was no danger in that direction unless the powder happened to go off.

We then went back to the cow ranch and loaded the three burros with mining supplies and grub which I had sent up, and struck out for our first trip over the trail with the animals. We got along all right until the trail gave way with Jenny, the old burro and John's special favorite. Where it gave away, it was at least five hundred feet straight down and just below Jenny. There was a mountain mahogany tree growing out of a crack in the cliff, and Jenny laid there on her side, loaded with a blacksmith bellows, fifty pounds of powder and six boxes of dynamite caps and fuse.

First of all, we drove the other two burros to a place of safety, unpacked them, took their lash and swing ropes, and went back and tried to fasten Jenny to another tree that was growing above the trail. We ran a line from that tree to a point of rock above. We made her fast to this anchorage, both bow and stern. Every time one of us would step down on Jenny, the tree would give something awful, but Jenny, bless her heart, would watch us and never move, and we worked fast.

John said, "Jenny, if you don't lie still, it will be Molly, toll the bell." And it appeared as though that burro understood everything John said to her. We started to get the pack onto the trail. John was certainly a genius. If we loosened the last ropes, everything would be over, and perhaps us with it. Oh, for an extra supply of rope. But first, we managed to get that cigar box of dynamite caps, and when we got that up and placed in safety, the sun shone brighter. Piece by piece, we finally got the pack up and in safety. As soon as we got the powder up, I wanted to throw the balance of the pack over, but John would not hear of it.

The next problem was how to get Jenny back up on the trail. It really looked impossible, as she was in the tree and about six feet below the trail. I can't describe how we did it, but I will say that Jenny was the best man in the party. When we would place any of her feet where we wanted them, she would not put any weight on them until we got hold of the ropes and gave the signal. We got down to the prospect and made camp and heaved a sigh of relief.

After John and I had been working several months running a tunnel and sorting the ore, we came to the conclusion that we would build an arrastre, and try and get some of the gold out of the rock. John said he could build it. I knew I could not as I had had no experience, but I could do some of the heavy work. An arrastre is a circle of stone about ten feet in diameter, two feet high, with the bottom laid in stone and clay of good quality tamped in the cracks. To prevent the gold from going down between, an upright post in the center with a cross bar running horizontally from the post, and about three heavy rocks around on the bottom rocks are so arranged on the cross bar that no one rock followed in the track of another, the drag rocks to cover the entire space in the bottom as they went around and around and around. Then a long sweep was fastened to this center post, and a burro was hitched to it. How foxy a burro would get—the moment you were out of sight he would stop if you were not yelling at him, then he would stop unless you were cussing him and throwing rocks at him. One pronounced trait a burro has, if you throw anything at him when he is packed or hitched to anything, he will stand perfectly still and clinch his tail tightly between his legs. Just why, I do not know. Finally, to keep the burro moving you would have to ride the sweep and threaten him with some kind of whip.

I have digressed in my description of the arrastre process of extracting gold. You broke the ore you were going to arrastre as fine as possible, the finer the more you could arrastre, put it in the arrastre, pour in water, just enough to make a kind of soup and keep it at about that consistency by adding water or ginding longer. You had a little gate on one side of the arrastre where you would draw off the top pulp or soup. I forgot to state that you added quicksilver by having a piece of buckskin tied over the neck of a soda water bottle and shaking it over the pulp as you would a pepper box. The quicksilver would come out as a spray through the buckskin, gathering the gold in the pulp and go the bottom where it would settle in the cracks and on top of the clay. You did not need to clean up for months, for if the ore was very rich simply add more quick. After running it with burros for some time, we found ourselves addressing each other with all the profane language we ever heard, and really had invented quite a vocabulary of new cuss words. We knew they were cuss words because we used them talking to the burros.

We were getting thin and did not enjoy our food, and we got to throwing drills and other tools at the burro hitched to the arrastre, cussing when we missed and cussing when we hit our mark. Our arrastre was built on a little promontory projecting out into Salt River and many times we would have to go into six feet of water to recover our tools. All nice enough in summer, but wait until winter!

I proposed to John that we build a water wheel, undershot, and run the arrastre by it, and he agreed right away, but remarked that it was going to be some job to get lumber in there. I told John that I would go and get Boody, who was our foreman on the Bark & Criswell cow ranch, and try to hire some young fellows who could swim, and we could pack the lumber twelve feet long to the river just opposite the Coffin Ranch and about eight miles above the mine, and there saw it in two. We would figure on making a wheel six feet wide and twelve feet in diameter. We would make the lumber into three lifts, bound well together, with a fifty foot half-inch rope attached and dragging from each raft, as there were very large boulders in almost every riffle and many rapids, one for Boody, one for the fellow I hired, and one for myself.

John said, "That is all right, but you want to be sure that you don't let the rafts get plastered up against a boulder in the rapids, as all h-ll couldn't get it off and you might get your head bumped pretty hard."

I said, "John, I will get back just as soon as possible." So I struck out afoot, got to the ranch that night. The next morning I got a horse and rode into Phoenix that day, ordered my supplies, hunted up a freighter. He loaded and struck out the next day, and the third day arrived at the ranch. In the meantime, Boody got the horses we wanted to pack and the saddle horses. We went over the pack outfits and were ready to load the next day, but made the river the next, spent the next day in getting our rafts ready and caching our supplies of grub, etc., to where John could take the burros and get them.

As we had no place to leave the horses, we brought along a Mexican boy who was working on the cow ranch with Boody to take the horses back. We started down the river with the three rafts, with nothing on but our overalls. In the quiet waters we would either tow them along with the rope, or pole them. We were as near together as was possible and we were getting along fine when just ahead we saw our hired man's raft plaster against a big boulder in the center of the rapids. He went overboard and for quite a while he did not come up. We could do nothing, as we were in the rapids. Pretty soon he came up and swam out. It developed that when he was thrown from the raft, the rope wrapped around him and the current held him under. As each of us had a knife, while under the water, he reached for his knife, opened it and cut the rope.

We fooled around all the rest of the day trying to get it loose and finally succeeded. We camped on a sand bar all night and it was pretty cold as we had no fire. Next morning, we went on and had no further trouble.

We could hear John talking to his burro long before we could see him. We soon built the water wheel, hitched it to the arrastre, but it would not pull it. We then commenced to build a dam across the river and finally got her going. The cable slipped off many times, but we finally got it regulated and soon made a clean up.

We recovered about eight hundred dollars in gold, but the mine was still in debt, so John and I kept it grinding until we had arrastred all of the rich ore that we had taken out. In several cleanups, we recovered about eight hundred dollars more.

We were a little ahead provided neither of us received wages. I went to town for more supplies, and upon my return the water wheel was gone, as the river had raised and swept the wheel away. So John and I continued to work at the mine.

Up to that time, we had had a single visitor, but a few days Jim Goodwin of Tempe dropped in on us, stayed over night and went his way. In a few days a young man came to the camp just before dinner, and I asked him to eat. He stayed with us about a week, and one night he told me that he was going to leave the next day, and I probably would not see him again; that there had been a big mistake made or he would have been down in Mexico before this; that his name was King Massey; that they were looking for him; that on a certain night, about a week before (he told me that night) that he and another fellow, whose name he did not tell me were lying under the Highland Bridge on the Goldfield Road—the ditch was dry—to hold up Bill Kimball, who, they were informed, was to bring to Mesa a bar of gold bullion, and then they intended to skip to Mexico. But their information was the bunk, as they waited there until daylight, and Kimball did not show up.

It was commonly known that Kimball brought in the bullion from the mine, but when, very few knew. Kimball had the boarding house, saloon and post-office at the mine, and the owner of the mine, who was Charley Hall, was a great friend of Kimball's, and as Kimball had to go up to the mine almost every day, it was very difficult to tell when he had the bullion. During hot weather, he almost always drove at night.

I have never seen King Massey since he left the next morning. In a few days I went to Mesa, and stopped all night at the Kimball hotel. In the morning at breakfast, there was no one in the dining room but Kimball and myself. He said, "Jim, I made a fool of myself the other night when I brought the last bar of bullion down." "How so?" "Well, I had about a ten thousand dollar bar, and as I approached the Highland Canal, I got a hunch that I had better go around. It was about two o'clock in the morning, and I paid no attention to it, but it persisted, and finally I turned out of the road, drove across the desert to the road a mile south of here, and then came up to Mesa. It was bright moonlight, and I just figure that I am getting old and panicky."

I asked him the night, and it was the night that Massey told me about. I did not tell Bill what I knew for obvious reasons, but it was certainly a queer hunch.

The Goldfield road is now the Apache Trail, and in packing in any lumber for the mine, we traveled along where the Apache trail now is, from the top of the hill at Fish Creek, up for about five miles, then bore off to the north to Salt River. Our mine was situated on Salt River, just at the edge of the water, and the Horse Mesa mountain looms over in almost a straight cliff for over two thousand feet. The Horse Mesa dam is just below about a half mile and the mine is now flooded. I wish to call attention to the distance between where John was prospecting and where we had every reason to believe the Lost Dutchman is.

This mine that John discovered while hunting the Dutchman is at least twelve miles off the course, and I think he finally hunted further away than that. You say, "How foolish." But remember John had been hunting faithfully for years, all alone, with his three burros. He would not see a human for months at a time. The natural conclusion, after thoroughly looking over the cliffs and crags, where his information led him to believe it existed, that he gradually expanded his area of search, until he really threw all logic to the winds and just went. At times, I happened to see John and his burros coming down the trail to the house, and hear the burros braying as they always did when they saw the granary which represented barley to them, and perhaps John had forgotten his mother tongue and was also braying.

To continue: John and I drifted on the vein until we came to the end; then sunk a winze about thirty-five feet and came to

163

the bottom. The vein became narrower as we sunk and the values less. John said to me one day, "Jim, you can have my interest in this mine, if I have any interest. I am going back and hunt some more for the Dutchman."

In a short time after that, I gave to Criswell, my partner, and Elmer Boody, foreman of the cow ranch, my interest, and I went back to the cow ranch. Criswell and Boody kept the assessment work up for a number of years and finally let it go back to the government.

John would hunt awhile, then go to work until he made another stake, and out for the Dutchman again. Although when John first started hunting, he had never heard of the Dutchman, but was hunting entirely on what Deering had told him.

One time, not many years ago, Sims Ely and a prospector named Wright and myself were running down some story about the Dutchman, and we stopped at Tortilla station on the Apache trail. We found John Chuning there as a station tender, where he had been working for about a year for the stage company running stages from Mesa to Roosevelt Dam, over the Apache Trail.

John was glad to see us, and said that he supposed we were out after the Dutchman. We said we were. He also said that he had sent in his resignation to the head office in Phoenix; that he was going to leave just as soon as they sent a man to relieve him, but the darn sheep men had stolen his burros as they drove through in the spring, and he had sent to Globe for some more; that he was all ready to pack up and strike out for the Dutchman, except that he had nothing to pack on.

We were gone just a few days, and upon our return we stopped to see John. He said that he had brought four burros in Globe and was waiting to be relieved, but that he was not feeling well. He said this time he sure had the mine and there was no mistake, and could he reach me at the Arizona Club?

I said, "Don't go off alone, John, if you are not feeling well." He said he wouldn't, but that he was sure he would feel all OK in a few days. A short time after, I heard that John had died at the Tortilla station. He never got away from his job.

I wish to say in conclusion that both John and I found many

GREAT REGISTER, PINAL COUNTY,

NUMBER.	NAME.	AGE.	COUNTRY OF NATIVITY.	LOCAL RESIDENCE.
547	Cunningham Williams H	34	United States	Wallopsville
553	Curry Jackson C	30	United States	Wallopsville
571	Crideau Julius	37	France	Naching
574	Clark George H.	29	United States	Pinal
582	Caraness Silas O.	46	United States	Pinal
593	Cann Robert	52	United States	Pinal
611	Chamberlain Roscoe H	26	United States	Pinal
676	Carell William	33	United States	Pinal
634	Culver Clark W.	33	United States	Pinal
640	Chuning John I	30	United States	Pinal
662	Carnlew Lewis	29	United States	Pinal
704	Corinelly Patrick	50	Ireland	Silverking
712	Crosley James	45	Ireland	Silverking
724	Casey Martin	34	Ireland	Silverking
727	Conway Edward C.	34	United States	Silverking
759	Cortland George	34	United States	Balti
766	Crosley William	60	Ireland	Casa Grande

John Chuning on Pinal County Register

sandals along the monumented trail, such sandals as the peons of Mexico wore, which were made out of the century plant fiber. Also around the caves near the water holes, were many picks and shovels, all old and worn. The handles would fall apart if they were picked up.

The finding of the sandals is almost absolute proof of there having been large parties of peons in there. It is almost certain that they were headed by Don, as the Superstition mountains was the Apache stronghold, and the last mountains that the Apaches gave up. In fact, the last Apaches were not driven out until in 1884.

Brownie Talks About John Chuning and Joe Dearing

The time came when my father suggested that I go to Tortilla Station and there endeavor to make friends with an old man

Death Certificate for John Chuning

named John Chuning who, it was said, had some information regarding the lost mine. I was told to invite him to accompany me on a search for the Lost Dutchman mine. Father informed me that Chuning was at one time shift boss at the old Silver King mine near Superior, and friend of John Deering, whom I have previously mentioned, had come to the Silver King with some very rich specimens of gold ore. He had asked Chuning to put up the first money for a first-class outfit and go with him to the mine. Chuning agreed to accompany Deering to the mine and also to invest several hundred dollars in a complete outfit providing that Chuning would wait about a month. This Deering agreed to do, and in order to pass the time more quickly and also to assist as much as possible in finances of the venture went to work in the Silver King mine. On his third shift underground a rock slide occurred and his legs were terribly mangled. One of them was amputated in an effort to save his life, and because of the lack of proper medical facilities blood poisoning set in. He died during the second operation performed a few days later. Before Deering passed away he called his friend Chuning to his bedside and endeavored to give him the directions to the mine. Chuning learned enough to give him a fair description of the mine's location, however, he made no effort to look for it until after Wolz's death. When he heard rumors of the rich ore deposit in the Superstitions he surmised it was the same property which his friend Deering had described to him. Prospectors of that day were no different from those of today. A man may come into a rich strike and unless he has several hundred dollars, or thousands of dollars rather, of ore on his person nobody pays attention to him or his claims. Chuning felt that his friend's was about average because the ore that Deering showed him, and though it was exceptionally high-grade, was so small an amount that it would not pan more than three or four hundred dollars in its entirety. When he learned of the passing of Jacob Wolz and of the many stories connected with the old German, Chuning realized he had passed up one of the major opportunities of his career as a mining man. He procured an outfit and went to *Tortilla Springs*, where he set up a permanent camp. I found Chuning to be a pleasant fellow of about 65 years of age. He was a wiry man in spite of his age, tall of stature, slightly bent with piercing grey eyes; they seemed to look right into one as he talked to them. Yet there was a slight twinkle in them that indicated a kindly disposition. As I rode into his camp, he was just clearing away the remnants of his evening meal. He looked up a little startled I thought, "Hello there," I said, "you're John Chuning, aren't you?" He walked over to me as I dismounted from my burro. "Yes," he said, "and who might you be?" "I'm George Holmes from Phoenix," I replied. "Not Dick Holmes' boy?" he inquired. "Yes sir," I answered. "Well, come right over and I'll fix you a bit to eat," he exclaimed good-naturedly. I protested that I could fix my own meal inasmuch as he had finished his and had cleared everything away. "Listen, son," he remarked, "no one can say they ever came to John Chuning's camp at meal time and didn't get a bit to eat. I'll have something fixed for you in a jiffy." With that he set about making over the coffee and frying some bacon. As he worked, he asked about my father and was surprised to hear that he was unable to hit the trail again. "I only met your father a couple of times, son, but what I saw of him those times and what I've heard at different times before and after meeting him, I think he is a real man." John Chuning must have known my errand, but if he did he never let on. He treated me just as if I was casual visitor and would probably move on tomorrow. The following morning I insisted that he prepare breakfast from my own store of food but he would not have it. He declared that I was his guest. It was only after I told him that I might remain there for a few days that he finally consented to share the food equally. Even then, as is characteristic of the old-time westerners and more particularly prospectors and mining men are, he did not ask my permission, feeling that if I cared to I would tell him of my own free will. After breakfast was over and all things cleared away, I broached the purpose of my visit. "Mr. Chuning," I said, a little hesitantly, "father asked me to come and see you about joining me in looking for the Lost Dutchman— we have some very accurate information that, coupled with what you might know, would aid us both a great deal." His immediate reply convinced me that he had known or strongly suspected the reason why I was there. "No, son, I feel that I am on the right track myself and you know how old prospectors are, we don't like to let anyone in on a good thing, that is if we can locate it alone." He readily observed the look of disappointment on my face. "Now don't misunderstand me," he went on, "I don't know anyone that I'd rather have in cahoots with me than Dick Holmes or his boy, but you see I've been here a long time and I've located a lot of valuable clues, and I'm going to find that shaft one of these days, and when I do, I intend to own the thing, lock, stock and barrel." I spent several days with him during which time I learned he was far from being on the right track. John Chuning was looking for an open shaft and the Lost Dutchman was covered over with six feet of timber. Chuning confined his search to the high hills in the vicinity of Tortilla Spring; he built ladders to climb up and down sheer cliffs and some of these ladders are still there. Before Mr. Chuning passed away in 1922 he told me some of the things that Deering had related to him.

168

Deering had, according to Chuning, built five markers from the mine to the big canyon to the south and he had made them all alike. They were made of long rocks, standing upright, supported by four smaller rocks at the base. *When he had gotten to the creek he cut a cross on a black willow tree which I have seen many times.* That tree has since been washed away. And I found three of the four markers, or five rather, which Deering erected. A photo of one of these markers I have. After this fruitless trip to enlist the aid of John Chuning, I decided to make a more systematic search. I then began a renewed search by starting out at Superstition Mountain, the main mountain of the range and gradually working north and east, thoroughly examining every canyon as I went. My various trips throughout the country always ended near a point where I discovered the tree stumps. It was unreasonable that the old German would cut logs and drag them into another canyon. To have done that would have required months of hard work. Yet, I reflected after my first enthusiasm had died down, I must find the rock house in order to locate the shaft. I confined a portion of my search in the hills to finding remnants of the Peralta party, but without any degree of success. I did find some old sandals and an old bit in a cave on one of the canyon walls. Whether these might have belonged to any of the party, I have never been able to determine. But their finding spurred me on to more prolonged searches. John Chuning informed me that a man by the name of Silverlocke and a partner passed through the mountains several years previous, about the year 1900, and not having any knowledge of the running fight between the Indians and the Mexicans, found numerous small pieces of ore. They continued their search and ran across several piles of the same rich ore. It is said that these two men took their find to Phoenix and received approximately forty thousand dollars for it. I have located the spot where the fight ended but as far as I know no gold has since been found. Up to this time I had searched most of the area south of LeBarge Canyon and incidentally, while on one of these trips caught my first glimpse of the dwarf deer. He resembled a jack-rabbit with antlers no bigger than the palm of a man's hand. He was not over eighteen inches high and would weigh not over twenty pounds. His body was a mouse color with spots about the size of a dime covering it. I have seen many dwarf deer since that first tiny buck. On one trip, I observed almost half a hundred in a bunch. When they saw or scented me, they would scamper off in every direction through the rocks. Later, after looking them up in the library, I learned that they are natives of South America, and related to Dik-dik. Others have seen these animals in the Superstitions but many people seem to think that I am telling customary western yarn when I say I have seen great numbers of them. I have seldom made a trip into the Superstitions that was not indelibly impressed on my memory through some experience. One time I found parts of a human skeleton that was so old that I did not go to the trouble to report it to the authorities. The skeleton was laying on the side of Crab Canyon, so named because a member of the party, which I was guiding when we discovered the skeleton, was so irritable that we did him the honor of naming the gorge after him. It was dedicated, place-carded and recorded as Crab Canyon, amid elaborate ceremonies in the presence of this crabby individual. The name will remain unchanged for evermore. Once when camping in LeBarge Canyon, near Marsh Valley, I began preparing the evening meal; the sun was just setting and as I had traveled quite a distance that day, I was very tired and hungry. After the cotton had boiled and the beans had been sufficiently warmed, I sliced enough bacon to round out a good meal; I had no more than placed the bacon in the skillet when I heard a noise coming from the top of an adjoining hill, and looking up I saw a man with four burros coming down the trail. In customary western style and being pleased with the thought of company, perhaps for the night, I added more bacon to the skillet and set out another plate and cup, at the same time gauging the coffee to make sure there was enough for two. Satisfying myself that everything was in readiness for the reception for my welcome guest, I awaited his descent from the side of the rocky hill. He seemed to be coming straight for my camp and as he approached to within hailing distance, I shouted out an invitation for him "To come and get it." He made no effort to halt, but drove his burros right past my camp, without one look in my direction. That was the first and last

Metallic breakdown of silver ingot.

Typical prospectors packing supplies.

time I ever saw him. I ate my supper alone. There are peculiar people who go into the Superstitions, most of them being eccentric prospectors who, having spent many years alone in the mountain vastness do not particularly care for the companionship of men. Some of them will walk for miles out of their way just to avoid passing another prospector's camp. There are others who possess the insane feeling that they are just about to locate the Lost Dutchman gold mine. And when they see others in the mountains, they feel that they are generally dangerous and at times are very likely to take a potshot at some unsuspecting person.

171

Chapter 10

Jim Bark's Physical Evidence

J acob Walsh said that the trail over the mountain to the mine was monumented with two small rocks. That trail and those monuments I have found over the mountain and down to a certain point; then the trail as well as the monuments became doubtful.

Dearing told Chuning that upon returning from the mine to his camp the first trip, that there was a willow tree growing alongside the trail and that while resting in its shade, he cut a cross X in the tree with a small hand ax which he was carrying.

Old Jake also said that the inclined pits in the mine were lined with mesquite wood. It must have taken an immense number of mesquite trees, as every trip they made it took more lagging, and one can plainly see that the trees have been cut with long intervals of time between cuttings. These, I certainly have found, as there was no other conceivable place the wood could have been taken.

I have come to the conclusion that the Mexicans have had three different trails going to their camp in Marsh Valley. The first trail ran along the east side of Bluff Spring mountain, about half way up the mountain, or as high as the bluff would permit them to make a trail. It was a very difficult trail to upkeep as there were many steep canyons crossing it, and in rainy times, boulders weighing many tons would rush down and tear the trail all to pieces. Judging from the growth of the trees in some of the short stretches of this trail that can still be seen, it was abandoned a good many years ago.

Their next trail was the one Deering found and followed, went up Havalina Canyon over into the horse country, down Peters Mesa to the Charlebois trail and thence to Marsh Valley (their camp) a roundabout way but always high up and fairly free from favorable spots for Indian ambushes.

The third, and their last trail was not found until a few years ago by the present owner of my old cow ranch, Gus Barkley, the most unlikely place for a trail I ever saw. It went up the southeast side of Bluff Spring mountain, and worked its way around the bluffs to the top of the mountain, a great many hundreds of horses and mules having been driven over it. As yet, I have not found positively where this trail comes down off the mountain, but I feel certain it winds up in Marsh Valley. This trail was traveled by all the late expeditions up to the mine, and it is almost Apache proof, and that they made this trail up the mountain and then, within three or four miles, several thousand feet down into Marsh Valley, their camp, is proof to me that the Apache Indians were giving them considerable concern.

About four years ago, there was an old well discovered in the upper end of Marsh Valley, nearly filled to the level of the ground. It was cleaned out by a couple of prospectors and proved to be about fifteen feet deep and very nicely walled with rock. It is my opinion that this well was dug by the Peralta expeditions and used solely for domestic purposes. When I first visited Marsh Valley in 1892, I thought it well named, as there were two or three nice springs flowing from under the bank on the west side of the canyon, and the whole little valley was green and marshy. No doubt the water there would become polluted by the numerous horses and mules accompanying the different expeditions; hence, the well.

There have been found a number of Mexican wood irons around Marsh Valley. A wood iron is a bar of iron about one inch in diamter, heated and bent so that it will fit over a pack saddle. Two are used on each saddle and are very convenient in packing long wood, as one man can do the packing. Also, numerous peon's sandals, both worn and new have been found,

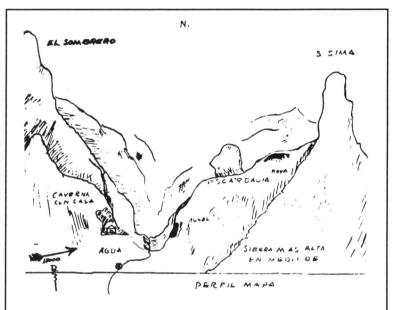

PERALTA/RUTH MAP

This map is probably the best known of all the various treasure maps pertaining to the so-called lost gold mines in the Superstition Mountains. According to Adolph Ruth, this was one of several maps that he received from his son after the latter had worked in Mexico. Erwin claimed after his father's death that this is the map the old gentleman had in his possession at the time of his death.

but always in caves where they were perfectly dry. As they are made from the century plant, moisture will soon rot them. These sandals are worn only by Mexican peons.

Numerous shovels, picks, etc., have been found, with the handles rotted away. At least, they fall apart when handled. Both picks and shovels showed a great deal of wear. There were a number of sheets of iron punctured apparently with a piece of steel like a harrow tooth (square), evidently used for screening dirt or gravel, and a number of sheets of iron not punctured. All were found in dry caves surrounding Marsh Valley, and all to the south, or along the trail which the Mexicans would travel in coming and going to and from Mexico from their camp at Marsh Valley.

George Scholey found a cross, and gave it to me, made of mesquite wood in a cave above Marsh Valley. It was set up in a cairn of stone, and it was bound together with rawhide, and had every appearance of being erected over a grave, evidently a Mexican of more than peon importance.

I also saw the race track that old Jake mentioned. It was two parallel tracks about one hundred and fifty yards long and located in Marsh Valley, about the only place in the Superstition Mountains that I know of that a track of this kind could be laid off.

Deering told John Chuning that on his second trip to the mine, he did not return to his camp the same way he did the first trip, but came down off the big mountain into a rincon, and there he put up four small monuments. "Oh, not much monuments— just a long slim stone stuck on end and four or five rocks laid around the bottom," and from there he went up the big canyon to camp, and "John, when I work that mine, I think I will be out the other way." John asked him why he put up the monuments. He said that if any prospector should happen to see the monument that he built at the mine, and then should happen to run across those down there, he would think that the same crazy prospector had been putting up his monuments down there, or if he happened to see these first, he would pay no attention, if he happened to run across the one he built at the mine. Those monuments have been found in the rincon.

I am proud to say that I can offer ample proof of all the above physical facts pertaining to the Lost Dutchman Mine.

Bark wrote at the end of this page, "To all who search happy hunting and a safe return."

Chapter 11

Apache Jack

There is no question in anyone's mind that the Apaches knew where the mine was. Story after story arose regarding favors done for the Indians by white men who then requested of the red men just one thing in return. And many tales came out of the camps which left no doubt the Indians probably wanted to comply; some even went into the canyons with that intention, but at the last moment, some quirk of fate, accident or just plain fear overcame a satisfactory outcome. Of these occurrences one seems more outstanding than all the rest.

By 1912 Jim Bark was in northern Arizona a good part of the time. Occasionally he visited with a friend living in Mayer by the name of George Scholey who was a miner by trade and later a blacksmith. Bark respected Scholey and considered him an honest man. So when the conversation got around to gold, Bark's interest piqued.

Scholey had made the acquaintance of an aging Indian while doing the annual assessment work for sundry nonresident owners of mining claims. Apache Jack was a pretty good laborer who had worked along with George for a long time.

The Indian lived in a settlement some 20 miles from the Scholey home, but, like many other red men living on the Verde River, would leave home for long periods of time to earn wages.

This Apache squaw has had her nose cut off for commiting adultery.

After they quit fighting, the Apaches slipped out of the range. They were considered intelligent and turned out to be good workers.

On this particular day the pair were working on a 10-foot assessment hole. The white man was tired, remarking, "Jack, heap work, little money."

Jack repeated the same phrase then asked, "George, why you no get mine?"

Scholey answered, "I look many times, but no find."

Later, sitting on the dirt mound having lunch, the Indian seemed to be considering what the white man had said. "George," he said, "Way off there," he waved his hand to the southeast, "much gold, one mine."

The miner knew Indians were unwilling to show a mine to a white man and even though he was surprised, said very little. Instead he picked up his tools to begin working again, finally saying, "I wish I could find that mine."

The Indian remained mute. The next day as they worked, Apache Jack said out of the blue, "George, maybe we go hunt for deer sometime?"

Scholey, understanding the workings of an Indian's mind, replied quite casually, "All right."

A few days passed. Within that time George had happened onto Jim Bark and repeated the conversation to the rancher who was naturally interested. They agreed the hunt should be planned and Bark would foot the bill. The journey was to take them to Fort McDowell on the Verde River, and then to the east.

Bark cautioned George against seeming too eager or being in a hurry. He told George that he had better be ready to go on a moment's notice.

Jack never mentioned the Superstitions but both the white men were certain that would be the destination. Eventually, they learned the hunt would take place on the far side of the Salt River in the area of the famous Apache Trail.

Shortly before they were to leave the Indian told Scholey, "Medicine man no like for me to go. He mad."

From the beginning George planned to drive his own car. He and the Indian made their first stop at First Water on the Bark Ranch, east of Goldfield. Leaving the car there, the pair set out on foot, toting a single blanket each and packs of food on their backs. Early in October the weather was ideal for camping out. They ranged at the Indian's whim only returning to First Water occasionally for provisions.

Now and then they took the stagecoach back and forth on the Roosevelt Highway, stopping for detours from the road in any area which struck Jack's fancy. After killing a deer, they spent two days preparing the meat for future use.

Two weeks passed. Jack suggested they return to camp, indicating that they would next hunt to the east of that place. Then, he mentioned they would have to climb a peak known as Black Mountain. Heeding Bark's caution, Scholey never mentioned the mine.

It took a long time until finally Jack and his white companion topped out on the summit which stands between LeBarge Canyon on the south and Peter's Canyon on the north—the two canyons converge at Mormon Flat—they were headed east. Suddenly, George realized Apache Jack was lagging behind and later described the man as "fidgety."

"George, I think we go back to camp," the Indian stated firmly.

Scholey was surprised. "Why, Jack. It's only the middle of the day. You're not tired, are you?"

The only reply was, "We go back, now, I think."

George became irritated momentarily making up his mind to have a showdown with the Indian. He had come a long way and had spent a lot of time and money and he wanted some answers. "Jack," he said, "Where's that mine you told me about?"

Apache Jack actually shook while silently waving an arm in an arc. It was a wide sweep, including both Tortilla Mountain and Weaver's Needle. Turning and hurrying off, the Indian rushed toward their camp without a word or a backward glance. They had gone some three miles before he recovered his poise.

Scholey hadn't known the history of the spot on which they stood until later, when Bark explained it. E. E. Wright, Sims' prospector friend, and Sims himself had made a trip there the year before. They had found some 40-odd Mexican firebeds, covering an area of about three acres.

A Mexican firebed is an open pit which has been completely warmed by fire. So warm, they say, that a man may sleep with only one blanket on the coldest night. To prepare it the peons took a shovel and cleared out a space about six feet long, four feet wide and say, six or seven inches deep. Then they filled the depression with wood, which would burn readily, and set it afire. When all of the wood had burned the charcoal was raked up to the surface on either side.

It had taken Sims and his friend a long time to discern what the depressions were. Rain and the elements had long since covered their original appearance. The charcoal and the number of the unusual places finally explained it as a place where miners slept. And, since the only mining ever carried on in that area was that of the Peralta-Lost Dutchman Mine, it followed that the users of the firebeds had been working Jake's mine, then known as the Peralta Church grant.

Apache Jack hadn't become edgy until they were on the northeast shoulder of Black Mountain which overlooked the plateau containing the firebeds.

After awhile Apache Jack stopped to rest. He and his companion set down to rest. The Indian was apparently ashamed of his refusal and became talkative again. "George. . .over there. . . ." He pointed to a place where two crazy white men had worked. They had taken out gold but were later both committed to the mental institution in Phoenix. "Over there, big fight one time." Then he told a remarkable story.

"A lot of Mexicans worked mine. The Apaches and Mexicans have no trouble, long time. Apaches stay near, have good food to eat. One time Mexican do bad things to Apache squaw. Bad medicine and Apaches fight."

George related the entire story to Bark later. "There were only two routes the Mexicans could take and these led south. The Apaches were practical fighters and had all the passes well guarded. Soon, the Mexicans had been defeated and found themselves cut off from an escape route toward Mexico. They turned northwesterly on a route which ran almost parallel with the range.

It was a running gun battle for two days. The Mexicans were being herded toward a western abutment of the Superstition wall.

Apache Jack was then a young brave of about 12 years. He lived at that time in an Indian village near the military camp of Picket's Post. The post was also near the ancient milltown of Pinal. After all of the trouble, the military moved the Indians closer to their posts to aid in caring for them and to keep them under a watchful eye, but when a runner brought word of trouble

Soldiers pow wow with the Apaches; later they came in and lived on the first military reservations.

within the mountains, the braves slipped away to join their brothers. Apache Jack went with them. After three days, most of the Mexicans were dead. The last group was brought down on the exact spot where the two men had been excavating. Those men had gone insane.

Jack stood and pointed to the spot, telling Scholey, "There, we kill all but maybe two or three. They get away around that mountain." He also said the Mexicans had mules with them. They would stand behind the mules and fire at the Indians. The animals slowed them up because they were packed with bags of ore. "Some mules were killed in fight," Jack said, "and the other mules went to Apache camp on mountain with flat top." He said the sides of this mountain were so steep there was only one way to reach the top. But on the summit there was water, and there the Indians camped in safety, eating the mules they had captured

Sentenced to death, Apaches in leg irons await their fate.

whenever they needed food.

Scholey was intrigued. "What did you do with the rocks that were in the packs?"

"We cut packs loose, leave on ground."

The gold had been scattered a long way. A king's ransom just left to the winds and the drifters who happened along later. Of course, this was part of the gold found by the men who later went insane. Certainly, not knowing the story, they had thought it was a bonanza. All the digging in the world wouldn't have netted Silverlock and Malm any more treasure. And, except for Apache Jack telling the story, an explanation would never have been heard.

Apache Jack must have been relieved to tell the ancient tale. He continued. The rest of the story added a new dimension to what had become a mind-boggling mystery.

While the Apache band was up on the mesa, they devised a plan which would account for the fact that it was exactly 40 years before anyone found the treasure again.

Another group of Mexicans, which Bark said later were probably poachers, had also molested Apache women. So a decision had been made to cover the mine—removing all traces of its existence on the surface. In true Indian fashion the squaws worked one entire winter. They shoved everything that was movable into the pit until it was full and then smoothed the whole surface over.

Apache Jack, friend to a white man, had made a fatal mistake. He had searched for the mine and came within a hair of telling his friend where it was.

Jack was without cunning and was slow thinking as many of the Indians were. He didn't have the qualities which made medicine men so feared. Leadership in the tribe was gained through fear and intimidation.

And, although Apache Jack hadn't exactly broken the rule, he actively disliked the medicine man. But the healer's admonition was firm. Apaches and Pimas alike had been taught if they showed a mine to a white man, a dreadful fate would quickly overtake them. They would die or go insane. Indians would never go near an insane man believing him to be possessed of evil spirits—a fate worse than death. The fear of this punishment is what had overcome Apache Jack just before he broke the tribal law.

On the drive back to Mayer the Indian asked a favor. "George, if me get sick, I send for you. You come quick. Then I tell you things."

Scholey, not realizing the seriousness of the matter, was offhand in reassuring the Indian.

A week later a runner from the Apache village appeared at the Scholey home. The 14-mile trip had left the Indian breathless but he gasped out, "Apache Jack sick, Mr. Scholey, come quick."

Scholey was many miles away on an assessment job; Mrs. Scholey didn't know exactly where he was and even if she had, there was no means of transportation.

When Scholey returned the following week and learned of the message, he hurried to the Apache village. It was too late. Apache

Jack had died soon after the messenger returned. Scholey knew a few of the braves. He questioned them as to the nature of Jack's illness and his symptoms. Scholey was forever after convinced that Apache Jack had died of strychnine poisoning, and no doubt the medicine man had been responsible.

Just before Scholey left the Indian village he was told that an old blind squaw, whom Jack had known for years, wanted to see him. She had liked Apache Jack and was very sad at his death. Having worked for whites in her younger days, she spoke fairly good English. She seemed to know what the entire matter was about and offered information to Scholey. She said she had once been to the mine Scholey wanted to find. Her words were, "Three big rocks, like wickiup," and she traced a sort of triangle on the ground with her walking stick. "You go by them—maybe, you go down on a rope."

Just then a buck came by and violently kicked the old squaw on the leg. The signal was a warning.

Bark and Scholey thought, as they later examined the evidence of this amazing story, that the blind, old woman might have been one of the Indians who covered the mine, "All one winter."

There are many stories of Indians offering to help a white man. Always they begged off or retreated before the promised confession. The medicine men weren't entirely to blame. Years before Spanish explorers had learned of the gold in the mountains because often the Indians had ore in their possession. It was immediately obvious to the Indians what their visitors wanted. They complied at first, but after they had told all that they knew, greed raised an ugly head. They were accused of lying and were tortured in an effort to make them reveal the source of the precious metal.

It was a common occurrence for the Spaniards to molest the Indian women, therefore, the leaders of the tribes made a firm rule and the dictum included punishment of death or insanity, which was forever kept.

There is one more story involving one of the Western characters who we have already met.

Aaron Mason, during his youth, had saved the life of a famous Apache chief, Del-Shay. It happened in the 1860s when Mason was prospecting in the country near Fort McDowell and Camp Verde.

As was previously stated, various tribes that had been captured were moved near military posts. In this case they were told to leave their homes along the Verde River and to move onto the Tonto Basin country. In one of the many fights that broke out, Del-Shay was wounded. Mason found him hiding in some brush and took him back to his cabin where he nursed the chief back to health. As a mark of his appreciation, Del-Shay gave Mason a piece of rich ore. As he did, the chief explained that he knew where the gold had been mined. He continued saying he dared not tell where it was, but added that when his time came to die, he would send his son to tell the man where it was located.

Some 20 years later Mason was manager of the Silver King Mine and had long-since forgotten the promise and given up prospecting. An Indian appeared at his office at the mine in Pinal. It turned out to be Del-Shay's son. "My papa is dead," he said. "I have come to take you to the mine."

Mason was shocked. Unfortunately, he had planned an important business trip to Los Angeles which couldn't be postponed. Telling the Indian of his problem, Mason arranged for Bob Bowen to take care of the young brave during his absence.

As an added incentive, Mason said Bowen could go along with them to locate the mine when he returned. Several days passed and then Bowen received a shocking wire. Mason had been killed in a runaway wagon accident in Los Angeles.

Del-Shay's son made no comment when Bowen broke the news. Bowen continued saying he had to take care of some business in Mesa first, but, "then you and I will go to your papa's mine." The brave remained silent and continued to be until a short time later when he and Bowen reached the Apache Trail. Then, he simply said, "I go now."

Bowen questioned him asking why? "Aren't you going to take me to your papa's mine?"

*A White Mountain Apache scout, Dandy Jim,
hung at Fort Grant, Arizona, 1882.*

"No," the young brave answered. "I told Mr. Mason I would take him to the mine. That is what I promised my father. I did not say I would take any other man to this mine." Once that was said, the Indian turned toward Tonto Basin and was never seen again.

Once again the curse had been fulfilled. Mason's life had been taken away before he could see the mine.

The reader must remember that Indians never told lies. The quote: "White man speaks with forked tongue," is not just a line from a B movie. Indians believed they would evoke the wrath of the gods for telling a falsehood.

Chapter 12

Adolph Ruth

T he fine line of fate moving through history drawing men's lives into its web has always intrigued researchers. Few stories have been so fascinating as the story which involved the man known as Adolph Ruth who disappeared while searching for the Lost Dutchman gold mine.

Perhaps newsmen leaped at the chance to excite the populace with a story of lost treasure because the United States was recovering from the Great Depression. Whatever the reason, the Ruth story received international recognition, and resulted in the birth of another legend involving Jacob's elusive ore.

Speculation regarding Ruth's disappearance infected even the most casual readers. Another interesting fact about the case was the involvement of Brownie Holmes.

Brownie, then living in the Superstitions, was a regular at the Bark Ranch. Of course, by now Bark had sold the place to Tex Barkley, a local cattleman.

In order to learn the background of the Ruth matter we must digress in time to the 1913 rebellion in Mexico involving General Carranza, a former governor of a Mexican state, and General Heurta, an upstart, whose efforts resulted in the assassination of Mexico's President Madero. The United States decided to support Carranza in his bid to save the country. Needing funds,

Carranza's plan included the sale of cattle to Texas but being aware of U. S. sanitary codes, the general hired an American, Dr. Erwin Ruth, to inspect the cattle.

Ruth was a veterinarian of some note. During his tenure, according to Bark, Ruth was riding south in Mexican territory when he was met by a squad of soldiers. In their center was a carefully guarded Mexican prisoner with his hands tied behind his back.

Ruth was not a stranger in that country. He immediately recognized the prisoner as a prominent insurrectionist named Gonzales. He asked the officer in charge if he could speak to the accused. Permission was granted. During the following conversation, Gonzales stated he would be put against an adobe wall and shot. In a last request he asked Ruth to do him a favor. The doctor agreed.

Gonzales wanted Ruth to go to his home, then accompany his wife and daughter to El Paso to try to get them into the U.S. where they would be safe. He said his wife's maiden name was Peralta. Gonzales also said that there were papers and two maps of mines in the United States hidden in his home, which he wanted Ruth to have. Of course, the doctor kept his word. Later, after depositing the widow and her child in Texas, he returned to his home in Washington, D.C., where he showed the maps to his father, Adolph. The senior Ruth was extremely interested in hunting for gold. He suggested that they go search for the mines. The family was dead set against such a venture, but the elder Ruth remained adamant.

As it turned out Adolph Ruth's stubbornness cost him his life. He could not have known that one of those mines was cursed. After learning about the man one could only speculate that he wouldn't have heeded the warning under any circumstances.

Erwin Ruth was a busy man who loved his father. He had an interest in mines and eventually consented to try to locate the first one. They planned to go to California when time allowed, but it was several years before they finally went.

Their search, although futile, resulted in the senior Ruth being injured. At some point, after being separated from Erwin, Adolph fell from a ledge and broke his leg. A Mexican doctor came to help the injured man and during the treatment employed the use of a silver plate. The accident left Adolph lame and for the rest of his life he walked with the use of a cane.

Unfortunately, Mr. Ruth's trip to the California Mountains left him with more than a bad leg, he had acquired a fatal disease— *gold fever.*

After time passed, Adolph declared his intentions to search for the Peralta mine in Arizona. Erwin said he was too busy to go. No fear or family objection could dissuade him—the old man's decision was made.

The preparation for the trip was thorough. He even went so far as to encourage a friend to accompany him on the journey from Washington, D.C., to the far reaches of the Arizona desert. Being a greenhorn, Adolph selected a time in late May 1931 to begin his adventure. The pair stopped at a filling station on the outskirts of town to get directions to the Bark Ranch. The heat and the roughness of the upcoming country caused his companion to balk. He decided to allow the determined Ruth to go on alone. They parted company.

By this time Tex Barkley owned the Quarter Circle U Ranch. When Ruth arrived there were several men on hand—a cowboy or two, some old prospectors including Brownie Holmes and Tex himself. Because he was unfamiliar with prospecting, Ruth talked candidly about his intentions. And, although no one will ever know if that alone cost him his life, it was certainly bad judgment which led him to discuss openly with perfect strangers the fact that he had a map.

As might be expected, the cowboys were only half interested as Ruth asked if there was a tall, sharp peak anywhere near the ranch. The prospectors remained silent and observant.

Tex answered, "Why, yes, that would be Weaver's Needle." He went on to explain that pinpointed the Dutchman's mine which everyone believed was near that landmark. The rancher went on to say the peak had been named for Pauline Weaver, a mountain man and trapper, friend to the Indians and whites alike, whose entire life had been part of Arizona history.

Ruth appeared excited, questioning the man at length about its whereabouts and camping spots nearby, etc.

Barkley shook his head explaining that no one would go into that country in June. He further stated that there had been no rain since March and that, "It's not good for any man to go into the Superstitions alone at any time."

We can only presume that Ruth knew none of the stories about the search for that mine or the rumors of the curse. And, given his reaction to advice, one can only predict it wouldn't have mattered anyway. The man, it seems, was intractable.

"Never mind that," Ruth replied. "Is there any water near that peak?"

"Yes," Barkley admitted reluctantly, there was always water in West Boulder Canyon, less than two miles from the Needle bearing a little northwest. And, seeing Ruth's grit, he added that the best route was the trail up Willow Canyon, the mouth of which was only a mile from the ranch. He explained that this trail led to a summit overlooking Weaver's Needle and then turned down to West Boulder. The pool was only a quarter of a mile or so down that canyon.

Barkley was preparing to get cattle ready for shipment. He admitted he was quite busy at the moment, but said if Ruth would wait until he had finished that chore, he would pack the man in himself.

Tex left as scheduled. As soon as he'd gone, the prospectors offered to pack the greenhorn into the Superstitions. That happened on June 14.

One day later the prospectors returned, saying they had taken Ruth to a camp.

Several days later Barkley returned. Upon learning what had happened he immediately rode into the mountains to look for Ruth—"On a hunch."

It was hot. The caliche crunched under Tex's horse as they made their way through bone-dry washes. Once the camp was reached, Tex saw that the man hadn't been there for more than 24 hours. Further examination of the articles left at the spot revealed that Ruth was wearing only light shoes when he left.

Barkley was puzzled. He and his ranch hand continued down the canyon shouting Ruth's name and firing their guns at regular intervals. When no one answered, they continued the search until dark before returning to the ranch.

The county line between Maricopa and Pinal counties runs right through West Boulder, therefore Barkley notified both sheriffs. By morning deputies had arrived for the search.

Although it may sound simple, the search would prove arduous and difficult. Summer heat absorbed into canyon walls radiated all day long and into the night. The air seemed to die and left men breathless. Rattlesnakes, the dreaded reptile of the mountains, had long since dug into rocky crevices, scorpions were embedded in damp sand hidden from view and all the animals had gone to higher country. Even the birds remained silent.

Weaver's Needle stands within three canyons. The canyons converge some two miles northwest of the spire, and at that point there is a ridge a mile long covered with dense brush. The ridge runs northwest and finally is lost in a right-angle intersection with LeBarge Canyon, which flows northwest to its junction with the Salt River.

One thing was certain, a man with a leather face, conditioned to heat and parching sun, might be able to sustain himself under these circumstances. He would know how to hide under deep shaded canyon walls, seek the cool seepage of a spring and stay out of the noonday sun. But it was evident from Ruth's attitude that he feared little and really didn't listen to the advice given by men who had spent a lifetime in those canyons.

Ruth's family was notified. His wife was beside herself with worry and his son immediately went West to start his own search.

There were many searches that summer and fall. By now the papers were full of the mystery and the matter had been given full play in newspapers throughout the U.S. All the mystique which surrounds the Dutchman's mine was reawakened.

At Ruth's camp Tex found the following letter:

My dear Wife and Children,

Yesterday, Saturday, June 13th, Mr. Purnell and Jack Keenan and I rode 3 burros and two carried my tent, bedding, fifty pounds of flour, 10 pounds of sugar, coffee, etc. I rode my burro until we got to this water. I didn't get off because I was afraid I could not stand on it again. Purnell and Keenan both got off their mounts and walked. It sure was rough, sometimes straight up and down. Several times my burro slid down stiff-legged and from six to ten feet.

We left the ranch at 6:30 A.M. and arrived here at 10:00 A.M. They at once put up the tent and my bed. Everything else was put on the ground. I was too tired and aching to do much. I could hardly stand up. The distance we made was between six and seven miles. I went to bed about 7:00 P.M. and got up at 6:00 A.M. It was cool last night, but the flies bothered you as soon as it was daylight. The highest yesterday was 93, but now, at 2 o'clock it is 94.

I am sitting under a big willow tree, water in front of me, water behind me. I made a shelf of sticks, wired them together and tied them with the axe. I put the bacon, chocolate, prunes, sugar, etc., on it.

I'll gradually put things ship-shape. Sometime tomorrow morning I'll prospect some. I left my car at the Barkley Ranch.

Love   A. Ruth

Ruth's son said later that Keenan and Purnell came back to Barkley's ranch to use his automobile to drive their women about the country and attend picture shows with them in Phoenix some 56 miles away.

He claimed they returned on June 18 and found Adolph's camp abandoned.

Sims Ely claimed Tex Barkley was the first one there. Whatever the truth really is seems immaterial, the search lasted 45 days and then was ended because of the July heat (which can exceed 115 degrees daily).

L.F. Purnell and, right, Jack Keenan, cowboy prospectors who packed Mr. Ruth over the southern pass to West Boulder Canyon.

W.A. "Tex" Barkley, veteran cattleman of the Superstition Mountains. It was from his ranch that Adolph Ruth set out on his ill-fated treasure search in 1931.

Sims Ely claimed Tex Barkley was the first one there. Whatever the truth really is seems immaterial, the search lasted 45 days and then was ended because of the July heat (which can exceed 115 degrees daily).

Ruth's son tried to hire pilots to aid in the search. He reasoned they could surely spot the man from the air. They all claimed the Superstition Mountains held great fear for airmen, and when the region was crossed, the planes held an altitude of more than 7,000 feet. Swift and sudden air currents are said to be ever-prevalent, occurring over and within those mountains. No aviator could control his plane and it would be suicidal for any to attempt the undertaking.

George (Brownie) Holmes, son of the man who sat at old "Yacob's" deathbed and heard the strange story of the Peralta gold mine, was part of the first party of searchers. He advised Ruth's son that he and an aviator had tried to fly the canyons in search of the mine and nearly crashed. They had been forced to abandon that flight.

Finally, a pilot named Goldtrap was convinced to try it and to photograph the area . He consented to attempt it at dawn when the air currents were at their lowest force. He refused to stay up longer than two hours after sun up. The photos were enlarged to 100 times their original size, as the parties hoped for a clue. None were found. The pilot was later quoted, "The profusion of pinnacles and spires reminded me of the headstones in a graveyard. The only trouble was the shadows were too deep and long for good pictures."

Later, Goldtrap said, "A man's crazy to fly over that mountain. It's no place for an airplane. There wasn't a spot as big as my hat that I could set the plane down in. If we had smacked, the ship would have been strewn over the tops of peaks to the bottoms of canyons. It wouldn't be necessary to go after us if we had crashed, there wouldn't have been anything left of us to find."

After that had been accomplished and at least 45 days of searching, the Ruth family felt that everything which could have

196

Dead Silence of Canyons Holds Secret of A. Ruth; Howland Joins in Search

Derided by persistent white men, Apache gods of thirst, starvation and death stood unperturbed among the towering crags of Superstition mountain today while puny humans resumed the search for A. Ruth, 65-year-old government employe of Washington, who entered the mountain fastness last month and became a part of the silence of the canyons.

Ray Howland, lost mine hunter who knows every inch of the rough Superstition country, spurned the search for Ruth. Howland set out after conferring with the son and comparing maps. Howland's map purporting to show the location of the Lost Dutchman, is identical to that carried by the lost prospector.

Indians entreated to aid in the search for Ruth rebelled after a two weeks groping among the impenetrable canyons, walled on each side by insurmountable stretches of glaring red rock. Ruth was given up —another victim to the silent gods of Superstition.

Then came Erwin C. Ruth, the son who gave the venturesome prospector a map supposedly showing the location of the fabulously rich Lost Dutchman gold mine. The son, skeptical of the Indian legends, penetrated to his father's last camp and there found a diary, some rattlesnake medicine, footprints and silence.

Continuing his search in the faint hope of finding further trace of the lost parent, Mr. Ruth proceeded nine miles up the blistering canyon and came upon a small lake. On the shores of this drying water hole he found more tracks which he identified as those of his father.

Unable to find further trace of the amateur prospector, the Washington searcher, undaunted by heat and thirst, took up the general direction of his parent's wandering footsteps and trudged surmounting obstacles of the legendary gods, and came out on the Apache Trail, near Goldfield.

Armed with only the diary, which contained no enlightening facts, Ruth began a careful investigation. The diary was dated June 14, the day before the Elder Ruth ventured deep into the hills.

Ruth learned that an elderly man who limped—his father—had been bothered by a leg injury suffered in his youth—had been seen along the mountain highway and had sought transportation to a hospital in order that he might receive medical attention for an arm injury.

Arriving in Phoenix, Ruth attempted to enlist the aid of the forest service observation planes in another attempt to find his father. A reward of $200 has been posted. Residents of the hill country near Superstition are assisting Ruth in every way. Indications are the hunt will continue for another week at least.

"I feel responsible in a way for my father's coming to Arizona," Ruth said. "I gave him the map which had been given to me in 1914 by a Mexican family I befriended. I never attempted to locate the mine described on the map, but gave it to my father because dreaming of finding the Lost Dutchman had been his hobby for years."

July 13, 1931

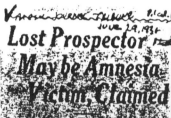

Lost Prospector May be Amnesia Victim, Claimed

Theory Advanced That When Aged Seeker of Lost Dutchman Mine Is Not Dead

SEARCH SUPERSTITIONS

Hunt Continues for Aged Man Missing for More Than Week

The theory that J. Ruth, 70, may be suffering from amnesia and is today somewhere safe in the Salt River valley was advanced today by members of the party searching for the Washington, D. C. prospector who came to Arizona by stories of the legendary Lost Dutchman mine.

Missing from his camp since a week ago today, searchers point out that his tent near the Weaver's Needle in the Superstition mountains contained his hiking boots and clothing and other factors pointed to the possibility that he had donned his street clothes.

A vivid description of the lost prospector—the best since his disappearance—was furnished by Ray Howland, noted prospector, who met and talked with the lost mine hunter shortly before he was missed from camp. Milton Rose, Mesa mining engineer, stated that he had seen the prospector.

Ruth's right leg is encased in a plated brace which is sometimes worn under the trouser leg. His street suit is dark with a light blue stripe and he insists on wearing the coat despite the warm Arizona climate.

On the basis of the new description and theory, county officers are keeping an eye open for the man in the hope that he may turn up in a valley city.

Lured into the mountains two weeks ago in the hope of locating the Lost Dutchman mine, Ruth was reported missing several days ago, and the posse of deputies sheriff from Florence and further afield prospectors living in the vicinity of mountains since have failed to find trace of him.

Led by a Mexican tracker, Capt. Roblas, five deputies searched the mountains under a scorching sun but found not trace of Ruth. Chester McGee, in charge of the deputies, returned to Florence last night, his clothes torn and his face and arms scratched by mesquite and desert bushes encountered in searching the canyons for the missing prospector. McGee will return to Superstition early today to resume the search, he said last night.

Ruth having saved and planned for his trip westward in search of the famous mine for nearly 40 years, came to the Salt River valley recently with a large assortment of maps showing the supposed locations of mines in the Superstition mountains. He hired a driver to take him into the mountains, established his camp, and requested his driver to return later with additional supplies. The aged prospector was missing from camp when the driver returned, and no trace of him has been found since.

Ruth has been employed by the United States government as a stock inspector for a number of years.

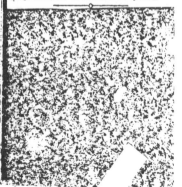

June 29, 1931

198

LEFT: Adolph Ruth around 1930

BELOW: Reward increased to $300 for finding A. Ruth.

BOTTOM: Headline from The Arizona Daily Star, July 21, 1931

ARIZONA STATE TRIBUNE

Reward for Missing
Prospector Increased

July 16 1931 p. 1 col 4

The reward for the finding of A. Ruth, amateur prospector lost in the Superstitions in search of the Lost Dutchman mine, has been increased to $300, the sheriff's office receiving a letter from a nephew of the missing man saying that he would offer $200 in addition to the $100 reward offered by the wife of the lost prospector. Although the search for Mr. Ruth continues, no success has as yet been reported, according to Deputy Sheriff Chester McGee, who is supervising the hunt.

P. 3 **THE ARIZONA DAILY STAR** JULY 21, 1931

c2 4-5

Heat In Superstitions Ends
Efforts to Find Prospector

Deputy Sheriff and Cattleman Unable to Stand Summer Temperatures as Rattlesnakes Hamper Search Among Canyons and Peaks of Range

been done had been.

Barkley and a man called Adams persisted. They were, after all, two of the cleverest mountain men. All their efforts failed. Even Adams' hunting dog, a bloodhound named "Blood," lay panting in the shade of the ranch house. His painful feet were doctored with mutton tallow to relieve the burns from running over the scorching rocks.

In one rocky canyon they found small, square pieces of tissue paper and tinfoil such as Ruth used to wrap around food cubes from his emergency pack. But there were no footprints—the land was too rocky for that.

Naturally the newspaper raised the issue of the curse and claimed Ruth was just another victim.

On December 15, 1931, the *Arizona Republic* newspaper sponsored an archaeological expedition into the Superstition Mountains to gather information about the reported sightings of many unexplored Indian ruins. This group consisted of E. D. Newcomer, *Phoenix Gazette* staff photographer; Brownie Holmes, guide for the expedition; Harvey L. Mott, *Arizona Republic* staff writer; and Richie Lewis, owner of the horses and dogs used. Odds Halseth was the archaeologist.

They were in the mountains for five days before anything of note happened. Then, on December 20, Richie's dog, Music, located the skull of Adolph Ruth under a palo verde tree in Needle Canyon. A recent rain obliterated any tracks near the find. Brownie Holmes picked up the skull to examine it and after noting two bullet holes in the temporal region, commented to the others that this was Ruth's skull and he had been shot.

Odds Halseth, the Phoenix archaeologist, was anxious to oversee the examination. One can only imagine that Odds believed he was the only qualified man to do it. It was silent for a long time. The trained professional fingered the object, finally stating that it was the head of an Indian and it was very old.

For those of us who were not present it is essential to know one bit of conclusive evidence: portions of skin tissue still clung to the bone and there were blowflies buzzing around.

George "Brownie" Holmes with the dog Music standing by the skull of Adolph Ruth just under the palo verde tree where it was located just minutes before this picture was taken.

It is very dry in the desert. That fact accounts for the preservation of human waste for long periods of time. One would imagine in that case, that flesh would reach a state where it would no longer attract insects. It seems safe to assume the uneducated cowboy had probably hit the nail on the head. And that fact was borne out later.

Brownie had been at the Bark Ranch at the same time old man Ruth arrived. He had time to watch the man and make his observations. He said the forehead and shape of the skull looked just like the man. E. D. Newcomer, the photographer for the *Phoenix Gazette*, asked Holmes to cradle the skull in his hands so he could take a picture.

Of course, by now a controversy developed between the members of the expedition over what they should do. Some wanted to continue the trek. Naturally, the newsmen were anxious to return to town where they could file what they considered a front page story. Remember, there were newsmen from three different papers present—oh, what a dilemma.

At last, a decision was made. The group would continue on to Charleybois Spring and spend the night.

Arriving there, Holmes and Lewis set about fixing up their camp while Halseth expressed concern over the security of the find. It wasn't unusual for coyotes to carry off bones from any creature. To prevent that from happening, he used baling wire to hang the eerie object in a nearby sycamore tree.

A later report stated it was damp and cold that night of December 10, 1931. Picture if you will, the campfire and the group huddled around it while Ruth's head danced overhead in the swaying trees.

The party left at 10 A.M. reaching First Water by 3:00 P.M. It was 70 miles from there to the ranch and another 56 to Phoenix. Since it was already almost midnight when they arrived at the newspaper, it was too late to have a pathologist examine the skull. Within two days, three doctors had examined the remains. All agreed it looked like Ruth. Halseth was adamant. He shipped the find off to the National Museum of Anthropology in Washington, D.C., to have it examined by an expert. Unfortunately, Halseth was out of funds. Offering the matter to the museum for experiment, Halseth hoped for a positive answer. The Science Service Bureau declined his proposal but by that time the Sunday edition of the *Arizona Republic* bore bold headlines which read: "SKULL BELIEVED THAT OF MISSING PROSPECTOR FOUND IN MOUNTAINS."

There are always men of science who are captivated by a puzzle and willing to freely invest time and efforts. In this case his name was Dr. Ales Hrdlicka, anthropologist and pathologist for the National Museum. His answer came by wire. It stated, "Skull unquestionably that of aged white man, recently shot possibly."

The *Arizona Republic* had gambled and won. The scoop set off a chain reaction in newspapers all over the country as the entire matter was rehashed. Of course, this set into motion new searches and by January 8 of that year the skeletal remains of Adolph were found in a small tributary canyon on the eastern slope of Black Top Mesa by Tex Barkley.

Brownie Holmes poses for news photographer after locating Adolph Ruth's skull.

The intrinsics of the case are fascinating; the lengthy search captures interest; the controversy bears discussion and the find is certainly worth mention, but there is one more magnificent matter yet to be discussed.

Before we add the O'Henry ending to this story, however, the reader needs to know the exact facts.

The Ruth brothers, furious by the refusal of local law enforcement to find their father's killer, were persistent in their quest for the facts. They pursued the matter with the National Museum. Dr. Hrdlicka worked directly for the Smithsonian Institution, a branch of the National Museum. He was a research scientist, dedicated to the most minute details. Later, he said the holes were definitely made by bullets fired at such angle that the victim could not have shot himself.

Twelve years later, Sims Ely interviewed the doctor who by then had retired, but who had stayed on in his offices to write his memoirs. He told Sims he not only remembered every detail of the case, but could discuss it freely. Then he added one more detail—the caliber of the fatal bullet, he said, was .44 or .45, and the shot had been fired from an old model Army revolver.

The authorities in Phoenix had refused to take action at the time of the location of the remains. They even refused to hold an inquest. A deputy sheriff, Jeff Adams of Phoenix, accompanied Tex Barkley on that final search. On a brushy ridge overlooking West Boulder Canyon, a considerable distance from where the skull had been discovered, they found the dismembered skeleton of the elder Ruth. Among the scattered bones was the silver surgical plate. In the pockets of the trousers were some trinkets which had belonged to the man and in the coat pocket were papers in his handwriting. There were no maps.

Ruth, as was formerly stated, was a precise man who kept a daily record of his movements and wrote detailed letters. His notebook, which was with the remains, stated the following: "It lies within an imaginary circle whose diameter is not more than 5 miles and whose center is marked by the Weaver's Needle, about 2,500' high, among a confusion of lesser peaks and moun-

Skeletal remains of A. Ruth sans skull.

tainous masses of basaltic rock. The first gorge on the south side from the west end of the range—they found a monumented trail which led them northward over a lofty ridge, thence downward past Sombrero Butte, into a long canyon running north, and finally to a tributary canyon very deep and rocky and densely wooded with a continuous thicket of scrub oak." The description was broken off at this point, but lower down on the page, was a single item,

"VENI, VIDI, VICI"

and then, hastily jotted down in pencil, Adolph's last words: "about 200 feet across from cave."

Sims said that this last fact caused him to decide to write his book.

This researcher has but one question. It has to do with the quotes in the notebook, just one sentence: "The first gorge on the south side from the west end of the range—they found a monumented trail which led them northward over a lofty ridge," etc. Why did Sims write "they found" and "which led them" northward. Was Sims taking license with the exact words? I doubt that. Something as important as that notebook would have been copied exactly by anyone so completely captivated by the mystery. And, if Ruth did say that why didn't he use "we?" One can only speculate about the words. No wonder Ruth's sons spent two decades trying to solve the puzzle because "Veni, Vidi, Vici" translates to "I came, I saw, I conquered," about 200 feet across from cave.

We are led to believe that Adolph Ruth found the mine and became a victim of the curse. His body wasn't found near it, therefore he must have been coming away from it when he was killed. Or was he forced to take at least two people back to it and then was brutally murdered. The theory was that coyotes had carried his head away from the place where the body was found. Maybe, but there is one more piece to the puzzle which is found in the last chapter and the reader should find it very amazing indeed. In that chapter is the story of Walt Gassler, a modern-day Dutchman hunter.

Jeff Adams, Music and Tex Barkley coming out of the Superstitions after locating Adolph Ruth's remains.

Walter Gassler had been searching in the Superstitions since 1934. He had come to know many of the regulars whose names flow through these pages. During those years Walt kept a diary which has never before been seen by anyone other than his wife. The result of his findings were in the diary which appears in Chapter 13. It also reveals a formerly unknown secret regarding Adolph Ruth's body.

Most of what has been said regarding the Ruth case came from newspapers clippings, Sims' book and Tom Kollenborn's monthly newsletter from the historical society. In comparing those with Bark's notes, however, it seemed that there were a few more facts which should be aired.

Jim Bark quoted Tex Barkley as having said that when he went to Ruth's camp his canteen and personal belongings were gone but his prospecting boots were there. After searching unsuccessfully, Tex finally moved the doctor's personal belongings over to the Quarter Circle Ranch.

Tex also supposedly reported that although Ruth said he had two maps, not much attention was paid to that by the cowboys because they were always coming into contact with prospectors who had maps to the Dutchman's mine. It seems everyone claimed they were going to find it shortly. In fact, Tex agreed that almost every cowboy who had ever worked at the ranch had at one time or another purchased at least one map to the famed mine.

[Some cow punchers paid as much as $10 for their maps. More fortunate individuals obtained their maps for less money; but they were equally valuable. At that time $10 was just short of half a month's wages. If a cow puncher was sold a map, say for $5 and he failed to find a mine worth a million he may never have invested in any more maps, but he was still confident enough to bet and lose his money on any other game of *no chance*.]

Bark mentioned something else which adds intrigue to this puzzle. After six months when the posse finally found the skeleton on the side of a small canyon about one-half mile from where the skull was found, it was mixed with some personal effects—a few silver dollars, a fountain pen, canteen, comb and various personal belongings. Of course, the maps were gone but so were his shoes. Bark made the point that the silver plate inserted in the bone in Ruth's right leg caused the leg to be several inches shorter than his left. The right shoe had to be built up to compensate for that inadequacy making it quite difficult for the man to get around in the mountains, especially in such rough terrain.

Bark also mentioned the blank checkbook which contained within its flap Ruth's notebook. Bark said, "I have a photostatic copy of this note and it had several quite large blood stains on it."

The reader already knows the rest of the story.

Ruth's murder was never solved. Unfortunately, a great deal

of time passed between his disappearance and the actual discovery of the complete skeleton.

As luck would have it, part of the mystery will be solved in Chapter 13, the chapter on Walter Gassler, the mine's latest victim, who kept a good diary and gave it to Bob Corbin before he died. It is included verbatim so that the truth is exact.

Chapter 13

Walter Gassler

A dolph Ruth's death brought forth a stream of articles in newspapers throughout the U.S., and later as far away as Australia, Europe and Mexico. But it was the article in the *Oakland Tribune* in 1932 which caught the eye of one Walter Gassler. So intrigued was the man, he headed for the Bancroft Library at Berkeley. After his first bit of research was complete, Walter regularly spent every weekend and vacation day in the stacks. The librarians came to know him and offered their help.

To read his diary one can see his quest became a library project leading the group all the way back to Father Juniper Sierra and Father Kino.

The project lasted two years. In 1934 Walt decided he knew all he wanted to know. At the same time he received an offer to become a pastry chef at the famous Arizona Biltmore Hotel. Unfortunately, when Gassler arrived at the hotel he learned that an old friend already had the position and not wanting to replace him, Walter declined the offer. Believing this to be an omen, the chef left for the Superstitions.

He arrived at Apache Junction, then consisting of a restaurant, gas station, four white cabins and an abandoned drug store. Pitching a tent next to the empty store, he camped and asked a lot of questions. In due time Walter learned of the Barkley Ranch and its personable owner.

The next move was obvious. Once Walt arrived, he was given access to all the information Tex had in his library. By now Tex had information from a lot of sources. All of the reporters who surfaced during the Ruth matter and enjoyed the Barkley hospitality had probably sent their own articles to the ranch. Tex was also gathering material from prospecting friends, locals and libraries. Walt refers to the Barkley library as a good source of material. He also mentions how disappointed he was to find so much conflicting evidence regarding Jacob and his mine.

Walt seems confused as he wrote of his doubts that Jacob and his partner had come upon the Mexicans who showed them the mine and offered to share it.

What a ridiculous story. Think! The Superstition Mountains, wild Apaches, claim jumpers—all kinds of wild animals. Wouldn't you have your guns loaded and ready at all times, right handy beside you for fear of your life? I am sure you would have your gun ready when strangers would approach you till they were out of sight. I can hardy understand how Herman fell for that story. [Here he refers to Herman Petrasch with whom he had made friends.] Also, you notice the story says they walked not climbed and all the other stories say it is in a very steep place.

As to the stories of the Peralta Mines which Waltz claims he found, he said that the mine existed in a canyon that runs north and south. Its peculiarities were potholes, hundreds of them, shortly after you leave Tortilla Creek and follow it up maybe a mile—you can't miss them and it will identify that you are in the right canyon. You follow up Peter's Canyon shortly after you enter Tortilla Creek. You will find the potholes as it enters the canyon properly. There, the story continues, the mine is about 1½ miles from a cave at the foot of a high bluff and a two-room house with a sod roof in this cave. This was the headquarters for the Peralta who worked the mine above. Which brings you up Pistol Canyon and Peter's Mesa.

Here you must remember that Rhinehardt and Herman, but especially Rhinehardt, spent a lot of time in Peter's Canyon to find that mine. That made me suspect that Petrasch knew more than he told and he must have heard it in Waltz's ramblings when he was dying, but just never got hold of the whole story. Of course, there probably were no names at that time for those canyons. I gave a map, colored topographical, I brought from San Francisco where I bought it and was made before Tortilla Flat was put under water by the dam. I think I recall it was called the Ray Triangle. Tex was crazy about it. So when I quit looking for the mine, I gave it to him. It probably still is in the family.

What made a story about a cave and a tunnel 200 feet across, that map that is floating around—don't say it is a Superstition Peralta Map and it might have some features of it alike. It could easily have come from all together some other part of the country. Especially since Ruth had several maps of different places and different mines with him. I am positive his Superstition map disappeared when he died, but it sure gave a lot of writers a bone to chew on. And look at all the stories that sprung up, everything around Weaver's Needle. Nobody was ever able to find the mine on those wild goose chases.

[Walt went on to say that Tex had told him when he was a youngster chasing cows back there around Peter's Canyon, that the cave was still there and had a few rafters and poles hanging there.] But there is still more to come.

The cave was very convenient to Peralta as right around the bend of the bluff there was and still is, a permanent water hole at the foot of a 10 to 20-foot drop of the creek. It is probably 6 to 8 feet wide. Maybe 8 to 10-foot deep and always has water in it.

[He then talked about the shape of the mine and the ledge and how you could walk and face LeBarge Canyon, which has a magnificent sight of the Needle.] It is like looking at a picture gallery and at the end is this grand sombrero, no wonder, if this should be the location, they named it the Sombrero Mine.

Walt had deduced that there was more than one mine. After all, Waltz claimed he covered it. "It is my opinion the Apaches covered it and Waltz never found it, so let's concentrate on Waltz."

Now, Walter talked to Mrs. Barkley who said she had known Waltz when she was a little girl. She remembered the German coming through the ranch and always bringing candy for the children. She claimed he was gentle; a man who would never harm anyone. She begged Walt to give it up and not become a "Dutchman-a-holic."

Walt had finally married and had a little girl. Mrs. Barkley was probably trying to save his marriage.

The woman also told him of the night Ruth went into the mountains. She said he had on a trenchcoat. It was drizzling when he came to the ranch. He showed her a manilla envelope and said, "I'll show you how easy it is to find that mine. I'll be gone one or two days." She further stated he started to show her a map and then reconsidered, saying he would show her when he got back.

After Ruth left, Mrs. Barkley was impatient waiting for her husband's return. When Tex did come back and learned of the trip, he immediately saddled up and went to look for Ruth telling his wife he was afraid for the man's life.

Walter said he believed that Waltz had found two skeletons of Mexicans who had not been able to get away from the Apaches. The Indians had already torn down that house to keep anyone from finding it. "Those Mexicans wouldn't come back, they knew the Indians would kill them." But, Walt did believe the Apaches chased Waltz away from the mine and he did leave his grub and mules. Walt further believed that while Jacob was making his getaway he came across the remains of the house, the charcoal pits and a pile of worked gold. And that is when old Jacob fabricated his saga.

At this point in the notebook, Walter Gassler wrote something which bears repeating. It attests to the fact that there were divided camps in the search. And, it also allows the reader to see how easily information was transposed in order to confuse and mystify the searchers.

"Old Holmes asked Tex one time if he knew of a grove of trees on a mountainside and if he did to let him know. Of course Tex knew the place he was referring to, but he told me (Tex) that he never cottoned to Holmes and never had any further

Walter Gassler in the Superstition Mountains, 1936.

contact with him. That was the time Holmes also told Tex the Dutchman still had several pouches of gold hidden back there. This also must have come from his deathbed murmurings."

Walt had a friend, a mining engineer by the name of Tom Reis whose experience consisted of 40 years in Chile, Bolivia, Colombia and Mexico. They came together in Arizona and Walt convinced his friend to come into the Superstitions for a look at the place.

Walt had found two pieces of quartz in the wash below the treegrove. Tom Reis said it would assay out at about $20 to the ton. They both admitted that wasn't worth fooling with, but it did prove there was gold in the area.

Tex and Tom Rels hit it off immediately, so much so that Tex offered to let the engineer ride his favorite horse into the mountains. Walt said later, he never knew Tex to let anyone ride that horse. Gassler never learned to ride; he made the trip on foot.

Leading the way, Gassler followed the creek bed up to the top of Miner's Needle. It was really rough. When they got to Bluff Springs it was filled with water even though it was August. Eventually, Tom asked, "Are you sure you know where you are going?" Cow trails leading here and there were the only sign that there had been life in there . The growth was wild and difficult to move through. When they got to Charleybois there was water and Tom seemed a trifle more believing.

In those days you could still see the sheetmetal shack, corral, some hedges and wildflowers put there by Charleybois himself. Walt was certain that all of that was wiped out after the big fire back there.

Now, they were moving toward Peter's Mesa in dense mesquite brush and thick oakbrush. It was so high Walt had to elevate his arms to walk through it. Walt said there was a path but it was barely visible and at every step he could hear the whir of two or three rattlers. Walt said, "Tom looked as if he really thought I was lost."

Finally, they got there. Walt expressed real joy as Tom explained the charcoal pits and the grinding stones nearby. The engineer explained that there had to have been 60 to 70 people working there for at least six months. But Tom definitely disagreed with Walt's assumption that the grove was the place where they mined. He took Walter over to the sloping side just beyond the crest of a hill facing south in Pistol Canyon saying that in his experience this is where it would have been.

When they arrived at Barkley's ranch that night, Tom told Tex, "If anyone would have told me that Walt Gassler could have made that trip on foot, I would have called him a liar."

Then, Tom talked to Tex about the huge field of stumps they found from the ironwood and mesquite trees which Tom admitted proved that there was a big production going on back there at one time.

Now, Walter Gassler's notes broke. His next heading said, "Ruth's goal and Waltz's dream fairytale."

I think it is impossible that one or even two men could ever recover this mine. When you think that 60 to 70 men worked there and what a hole that must have been—well. Then, the Apaches covered it. One man could probably work two or three years and just scratch the surface. I feel silly now that I thought I could do it alone. Just listen to what Tex told.

An elderly Indian woman Tex knew well told him at one time she remembers when she was a little girl her mother took her with her and a small tribe of Apaches into the mountains to cover up a mine. She said they had a camp on top of small mountain, on the side below it was a big cone-shaped mine with a pole in the middle and chain attached to it so one could grade the chain and walk around the small path down to the pit of the mine. Close to the mine there were three large stones (boulders), tepee shaped. She said they threw the tools and chains down into the pit and then, started to cover the mine. It took six moons and the women did all the work. The men hunted and made mescal up at the camp. Tex said you could still see the place where they made the mescal. Then, the old Indian said they planted young trees of mountain laurel and cottonwood over the area to make sure it wouldn't be found again. They also blended the surroundings to make it look natural. That solves part of the Puzzle. I also think they tore part of the cabin down. They didn't seem to care about the charcoal pits. They probably used the grinding stones to grind up their corn.

Walt, at this point, described what Sims had said in his book about the Indian woman who was a friend of Apache Jack's. he said, "The tool and chains are probably buried too deep to be reached by a metal detector."
Here Walter Gassler complimented himself.

It still amazes me to think, how, as a complete greenhorn from San Francisco, I could have found that mine the very first time out.

Tex explained to me at the ranch all the problems. He warned me not to drink any stale water, to watch out for snakes, and to avoid any human beings back there as much as possible. So I took off. I found Charleybois Springs and then went up from there. It was pure luck. Somehow I got to Peter's Mesa then, went on top of that ridge, went to the northern end down off it and kind of circled around on the bottom southerly and came to the bottom of a wash running south. Then I saw beside the wash a big pile of rocks, kind of square looking and thought it was odd. Glancing up on the hillside above, I saw a grove of trees and three big boulders. And, I knew I'd made it. Further investigation led me to the charcoal pits with the grindstones laying around. My heart jumped out of my mouth; hell, I was at the Lost Dutchman. But, the task proved too much in the end. I had to give it up. Oh, I dug alright but to no end. There was one hole already there and I thought Tex, maybe, had already tried it.

You must remember I could only prospect in summer. I had to work in wintertime. No water up there and it was two miles to Charleybois Spring and a long way to the watering hole in Peter's Canyon.

Mrs. Barkley told me later that Tex had said, "that greenhorn will never find it." And, when she found out what he had done she really scolded him. When I did find it, he sure became a different man.

Then, I went up to Bluff Springs and found that cave. And, it is a funny cave, not very big. You can crawl comfortably in there. It is about 15 to 20 feet deep and has a chimney hole up through it, straight up. You can crawl up it or climb a big boulder above and see down in. The top blends right in with the plateau. You would never see it is there.

On the bottom there is a large, thick bush growing absolutely innocent. The reason I noticed it was I was sitting nearby and thought I saw a dark blotch. It couldn't have been a shadow as the sun was at the wrong place. So I ambled over to it and poked it with my walking cane, which I always have with me, and I went right through. I almost fell down. I poked some more in case there were rattlers in there. But, I got no response and crawled in. Another funny thing about the cave is if you put anything light down like papers or leaves or light sticks at the entrance and the top is open, it sucks them right up and out. Maybe the Indians used it for smoke signals or the Mexicans. When I got back to the ranch and told Tex he was dumbfounded. In fact, he saddled right up and went out there. After that, we were intimate friends.

All the stories about Dutchman, Ruth, and the Peraltas I got from him. In the late evenings after supper we would go out and sit awhile on that hill rise as you came around the bend in the river. We would roll a smoke and talk a little while. I wish I had known then what I know now; we might have solved the puzzle while he was still alive. I still feel bad today that I couldn't have done better for him and his belief in me.

Now I know those stones I found in the wash must have been discarded stones from that rock house.

Tex also told me about a cave on Horse Mesa. I looked for it but never found it.

There was an old prospector in Tortilla Flat; they called him Monument Smith. I got to know him real well. He wanted to know about that cave. I told him all that Tex said. Monument wanted me to question Tex more but I said, "If Tex tells you something and that's all he tells you, you'd better leave it alone." Then, there was Anderson, bad character. Run into him once and he asked me. Told him, "Don't know." Billy Martin was there fur trapping in the winter and guiding. Met him after he got rid of his gang and was cleaning up his camp down below Charleybois. He asked me if I saw his burros. I said yes, they were just above Charleybois and above the mesquite flats. I told him to be careful—I just passed two rattlers in there. He said, "The hell with them, I'm not going through that. They'll come back, I'd rather wait." We walked to his camp and talked. I really liked him. Before I left he gave me a bottle of old Taylor, said he don't drink. I didn't either, but I gave it to Tex; he grinned from ear to ear.

I told Tex about all the people who wanted to know about that cave. Tex said, "I was up on Horse Mesa early one morning and I followed a bunch of wild horses, they led me right in there. Nobody would've ever thought it'd be in there. But, one time I was tramping all the way down LeBarge to Canyon Lake, I had a real powerful pair of binoculars. When I was by that willow marsh I saw up on the cliffs what looked like a cave, I guess, I filed it away in my memory." Then, Tex said you could look 1,500 feet straight down in the river. I thought he meant the Salt. But, when I read Barnard's book where he describes that cave from where he could see the Weaver's Needle, I realized that Horse Mesa to Barkley was Malpais Mountain Flat and there is that cave. Wild horses from up there even today I suspect. When I was up there in 34 to 42 some 50 to 60 horses with a white stallion came every morning. So, the mystery is finally solved. I have not been there yet. I want to see if Barkley left any kind of hint there for me. He was always playing jokes on me.

He has destroyed or dismembered all the grindstones, has scattered them and turned them upside down so you never realize what they are. And, since the pits are all covered you don't know where they would all come from. He must have even tried to tumble the boulders down the slope with a lasso since the middle one is broken off about a third of the way down. I am sure he would figure I would know and understand. I sure do, Tex.

One evening he revealed to me that originally only two boulders were up there by that mine and the Peraltas found another one just like it and put it there for a marker. I

Weaver's Needle.

asked him, "How do you know?" He grinned and said, "Greenhorn, if you look under them there stones you will see that two of them have no growth of any kind coming from underneath while the third one has all kinds of them. So, the first two are natural and the other was put there."

Then came the time when I told Tex, I just could not keep up. Either I would have to give up prospecting or my family. He was shook up some; then, that evening, he told me about

Ruth. He said he knew he was dead. He said he looked for a couple of days and then, got serious about tracking. It had rained back there before Ruth went in and he found his cane prints. He said he followed up to Peter's Mesa and said Ruth found the landmark. He said he must have been tired and when he saw the grove of trees on the slope he headed for them.

He sat on a protruding rock, rested and looked around and saw the three boulders in front of him and knew he had come to the end of his search. He must have taken out his notebook and wrote, "VENI, VIDI, VICI." In the meantime, whoever was his guide got impatient and told him, "Let's go." Ruth realized he would die when the guide knew the location and he would die if he did not. Then, he must have realized what he had done by writing those words which meant, "I came, I saw, I conquered," so he added "two hundred feet across from the cave" which would surely be misleading.

That is my guessing. Tex claims the guide put the gun to the side of Ruth's head and told him to get going. He must have gotten excited and pulled the trigger, took the map and disappeared. Tex found the body, got a mule and Tom Dickens, a cow puncher; they put his body in burlap and transported it to Black Top Mesa hoping it would be found there. Again, I asked him why. He explained that a few years ago somebody claimed they found the Lost Dutchman and about 200 people came stampeding back there and scattered his "Cattle to Kingdom come—clear up to four peaks." It took about 60 days and extra cowhands to recover all the cattle and he said, *"not ever again."* I sympathized fully with him.

I also figured Tex was baiting me. Well I horsed around another week and I guess, the last day, I prepared to go into the hills about 8 A.M. on Saturday. He came out with me to the road leading to Miner's Needle. He looked me straight in the eye, then I saw he came to a decision about something. He said, "Wait a minute, Walt, I will show you positive proof that the mine is there." He strode towards the house, stepped on the veranda just as Bill, his son, and Brownie Holmes came around the house corner up from the smithy, tipsy already. Tex saw them, turned around, came back and said, "I don't want them to see it. I'll show you some other time."

What was it? I'm sure it was the map. But, I figured it could have come from the notebook or gold he had found up there. Wish I knew what it was.

That was the last time I ever saw Tex.

I went away to Tennessee for a number of years. When I came back I visited with Mrs. Barkley when I had time again.

I started to collect information again and came to all these conclusions. I also remembered something else he told me that makes me think he told me the truth about finding Ruth's body up there on Peter's Mesa.

He told me when he found the body it was laying on its side, not the way a body falls forward, he said the killer had the pistol actually right to his head—flush. Then, he pulled the trigger so that it knocked Ruth sideways and he died that way and laid that way. That's what makes me think he actually found the body shortly after death. He also said to me that when Brownie found the skull and he took in the searching party, he took them right to the bottom where he knew the body was. Brownie said, "You fellows go up this way and I'll go up over these rocks." Tex said Brownie knew they could not miss the body and they didn't.

Still another time Tex told me about an Indian that owed him a favor. He said the Indian told him about a gold mine and would take him there. They went up to what is now called Peter's Canyon, clear up to the cave and the creek obstruction around the bed from there. As they approached this place, Tex said the Indian actually froze, stared up the canyon like he seen a ghost, grabbed Tex and told him "up there, take right hand canyon." He fled and Tex never saw him again.

You will also notice that whenever they claim they found the mine or gold it was always coming up from the north going south. I was forever trying to find them potholes in that elusive canyon but always workin' up from the south I never found it. Then I ran across that old map at the Phoenix Library that showed the old Spanish trail that branches off from Tortilla Creek and goes into Sheep Mountain, Geronimo's Head to Malpais Mountain into Peter's Canyon up to Peter's Mesa and Charleybois Spring, then finally, I went to Tortilla Flat up Tortilla Creek to

223

find that trail, missed it somehow, but came on Peter's Creek and followed it up the canyon to the cave and made my camp there. Then I was going up to Peter's Mesa, but next morning it was black and cloudy and a heavy storm forecast and I did not want to get trapped in that canyon so I beat a hasty retreat. And then on the way out of that canyon and a short distance down Tortilla Creek on a slight bend of the river, I saw the start of that old trail. It was quite visible coming that way. While on the way up you miss it if you aren't careful. Don't even know if it's possible today. Maybe Tom Kollenborn can find it on his horse.

That trail should lead you within a few hundred feet of that cave on LeBarge Canyon side of the mountain. There you can look 1,500 feet down to the river. You should come out a short way south of the other cave and the fall according to Barnard's story; Waltz stayed at the cave on LeBarge side of the mountain. He watered his burro on the old water hole that would surely be that large pothole which always has water and is only minutes away from that cave. This trail gave Waltz also the option of going the way of Tortilla Flat to Phoenix or the other way south by Charleybois and Bluff Springs or Whiskey Springs. He could alternate and confuse his followers.

Surely there must have been some certain marker or sign—something to identify the exact or close location to the mine. Just to say 2½ to 5 miles from the Weaver's Needle just would not have been enough for anybody, for a general direction. Yes, but since so many places back there look so much alike and identical, it just would have been better identification and that might have been the oral secret and final clue to the map Ruth was carrying. Ruth's son said he had some personal clues not on the map. Will this all bring the search to an end or are there some more loose ends? Maybe we will find out more in the LeBarge facing cave?"

And so ends Walter Gassler's notes. Walter never said anything about dates. He disappeared from the Superstitions for many years, but later became the curse's most current victim.

Chapter 14

The Last Victim

A rizona's Department of Law in the state's capitol complex, sprawls along an entire city block, just a stone's throw away from the decaying cemetery where Jacob Waltz is buried. The man who heads that department, Attorney General Bob Corbin has searched for the mine since his 1957 arrival in Phoenix. His interest in the mine is well known through numerous articles in magazines and newspapers; radio talk shows; speeches; television documentaries; and one episode of the television favorite, Unsolved Mysteries, a study on the Superstitions and the lost mine, which included Tom Kollenborn and Bob Corbin.

The attorney general's private domain is filled with antique oak furniture and private memorabilia depicting the Old West. At exactly noon on December 12, 1983, his secretary ushered in his next appointment. The visitor was Walter Gassler.

Over a period of years Corbin has been inundated with requests from reporters, photographers, movie producers, businessmen, prospectors and a few characters whose mentality was questionable, to take them into the range. It was not uncommon to receive calls from around the world from people claiming to know where the mine is. And since the attorney general enjoys talking about the mine more than he does eating, he often schedules those appointments during his lunchtime.

Walter's age showed on a wrinkled, honest face, but his weathered body moved with rigid determination. In his hand he carried an orange, line-ruled notebook. After introductions, for they had not met before, Mr. Gassler proceeded to tell the lawyer that he had looked for the Dutchman since 1931. He was close to finding the mine, he said with complete sincerity, and really felt he needed the security of some trustworthy companions. He further stated that he knew Tom Kollenborn and Bob were friends and would like them to share his experience and the gold.

Corbin is noted for being down to earth and never openly argumentative. Besides, he told Tom Kollenborn later, he liked the old man. However, it was a fact that hundreds of people over the years had made that same statement.

Gassler was no fool, he had anticipated that reaction and being prepared for the eventuality, had brought with him a diary of his experiences in the Superstitions. And, to further plead his case, he presented his notebook to the attorney general saying, "I'd like you to read these notes. If after you have read them, you do not believe I know what I am talking about, I will not trouble you again."

Bob said, "The man seemed astute and after having read his notes, I have no doubt his opinions were sound. But, whether he has actually located it still has to be determined."

Tom Kollenborn knew of Gassler. Tom made it his business to know everyone who went into the mountains with any regularity. He also knew that Gassler had been a friend of Tex Barkley and Tom and Tex were also close friends. In fact, Tom considered the cowboy rancher to be a second father. If Gassler was good enough for Tex, in true Western style, he was good enough for Tom. However, they'd never met and Tex was now dead.

A tentative trip had been discussed but, for one reason or another, never came about.

In May of 1984 Tom Kollenborn received a call from Walter Gassler. It was Sunday evening and the old man seemed anxious. He asked Tom if he knew where he could get hold of Bob

Bob Corbin (left) in the Superstitions being interviewed by radio announcer George Scott (right).

*Tom Kollenborn and Crow pause in the Superstitions
with his dog, Duke, close by.*

Corbin. Tom told him his friend was enjoying a brief vacation at his cabin in Prescott and that there were no phone lines on the attorney general's mountain. Gassler seemed upset. He said he had finally figured out the puzzle and asked Tom if he could accompany him into the mountains the following day. Tom said he was truly sorry but business would prohibit him from doing so. "Besides," Tom told Bob later, "how many times have we heard that same story over the years."

On Thursday of that week Tom Kollenborn called Bob Corbin's office to tell the attorney general that Walter Gassler's body had just been found on the trail above Charleybois Springs. There was to be a coroner's inquest but it looked as though he had died of a heart attack. Of course, both men were shocked and felt remorse that they hadn't been able to accompany the old man on what was to be his last journey.

That weekend a man appeared at Tom Kollenborn's home. He introduced himself as Walter Gassler's son. Tom invited the man in and after exchanging pleasantries the man brought out some rich gold ore. He said it was in his father's backpack when he was found on the trail. Tom was shocked. But, maintaining his usual dour facade, he examined the ore and later said it looked exactly like the gold which came from under the Dutchman's bed. The man listened patiently. After a bit he said, "I understand that my father gave his notes to Bob Corbin, is that true?" Tom nodded, saying little, in true cowboy fashion. It was apparent the man wanted those notes back. Tom suggested he call the attorney general at his office in the state capitol, and the matter was left right there.

A week later Tom called Bob to see if he had heard from Gassler's son. Bob said no, but he would gladly give the notes up to the family; he felt that was only fair.

Again, fate seems to work in strange ways.

Tom Kollenborn is invited regularly to show a slide presentation of the Superstitions during which he tells the tales of the Dutchman's mine, exotic tales of the 68 murders and wonderful stories of the characters who live and some who have died in those canyons. The slide show is so well accepted that it has traveled to Europe and throughout the U.S. This particular show was down in Florence, Arizona, the county seat of Pinal County, home of the old Silver King, Tom Weedin and the place where the swamper was last seen. Right after the show Tom was approached by a man who introduced himself as Walter Gassler's son. The fact that Tom is a stoic probably saved him from gaping. The man who stood in front of him was well-dressed and polite but bore absolutely no resemblance to the person who had come to his home with the ore. The man proceeded to make the same request about the diary and was given the same answer as Tom had given to the first man. Only this time, Tom went right to a phone to call Bob Corbin.

Two days later Bob received a call from a man claiming to be Walter Gassler's son. Bob said he was busy and would return the call shortly, then asked for a home number. That telephone number was the same one Walter Gassler had given him. This time, it appeared, he had the right son. Bob Corbin was also impressed with the fact that the man said, "I don't want to take the notes away from you; my father wanted you to have them.But, if you could Xerox them and give them to me for our family mementoes, I'd appreciate it." Of course, the attorney general complied.

The pair met for lunch. During the course of the meal, the son was politely questioned as to his father's effects which were brought into town by the sheriff's office. Bob said, "Ron, did you find your dad's backpack?"

Ron looked puzzled and answered rather hesitantly, "Why, no. It was listed on the paper which recorded his effects but when I picked them up it wasn't there."

Bob Corbin later said he believed the man was sincere.

Had Walter Gassler gone in alone, discovered Jacob's secret, extracted some ore, hurried away in fear and had a heart attack on the trail? The inquest confirmed he died of a heart attack. He was in his 80s and surely a shock of that magnitude might have killed a younger man. Or, was he followed by some unknown person who stalked him and then tried to force him to take them both back to the mine. Or, is it a simple fact that someone found the pack and removed the ore? Was the gold taken from the pack on the trail? Or did someone in the sheriff's office take it in the excitement of the moment? Whatever happened remains a mystery.

Tom identified the gold. He has looked at a lot of specimens in his day—he has a degree in geology—he is not a novice. He stated the gold was almost identical to that which came from under Jacob's deathbed.

All of the above are facts which cannot be disputed.

Walter did go into the Superstitions on that last quest; Walter did say he knew where it was and Walter died in possession of valuable gold ore.

The following is an affidavit from Attorney General Bob Corbin

sworn to on April 10, 1985.

<u>AFFIDAVIT</u>

This is to certify that I am Bob Corbin, Attorney General of Arizona. I have held that office since 1979.

My hobby is searching for the Lost Dutchman Mine in the Superstition Mountains which I have done since 1957.

Approximately three years ago I had the opportunity to be shown ore samples, documents and jewelry made from said ore which is owned by an Arizona businessman. This individual obtained these valuable items from Brownie Holmes, son of Dick Holmes, who was present in the home of Julia Thomas on October 25, 1891 when Jacob Waltz died.

I have in my possession an hour long tape made before Brownie's death which states that he gave these items to said businessman. He further states that the Dutchman gave these items to his father which were stored in a candle box under Jacob's deathbed. I have seen the report on said ore which was assayed at Goldman's store by Dick Holmes. This report states that the ore assayed out at $110,000 a ton. Gold was selling for $20.64 an ounce in 1891.

With the items were shipping papers indicating some of the ore had been sent to a jewelry company in San Francisco in 1892. A request accompanied it directing the jeweler to make a matchbox, ring, tie pin and cuff links from the ore. I have also seen the papers shipping this jewelry back to Phoenix.

I had permission to photograph the matchbox which will be used in this book. I have seen the ring made from this ore, but I have not seen the tie pin or the cuff links. This is the first time the Dutchman's Gold has ever been photographed.

I was told by the individual who owns the assay report, jewelry and ore that this ore had been sent to the University of Arizona, School of Mines which has samples of gold ore from every known Arizona gold mine to see if the ore could be matched up. I was further told by this individual that the University of Arizona, School of Mines had informed him that this ore came from an unknown source.

The reason that I cannot name the individual who has the ore, jewelry and documents is that I gave my word I would never divulge his name without his permission if he would show the ore to me which, as stated above, he did.

Further affiant sayeth not.

Bob Corbin
BOB CORBIN

SUBSCRIBED AND SWORN to before me this 10th day of April , 1985.

Kathleen M. Copus
Notary Public

My Commission Expires:
11-9-88

BC:kmc

The following is an affidavit from Tom Kollenborn sworn to on April 13, 1986.

AFFIDAVIT

My name is Tom Kollenborn and I reside in Apache Junction. I am an administrator with the Apache Junction school system and the curator of the Superstition Mountain Historical Society.

I started searching for the Lost Dutchman Gold Mine in the Superstition Mountains in the early 1950's, as had my father before me.

Approximately three years ago I had the opportunity to be shown certain ore, documents and jewelry which are owned by an Arizona businessman who had received the ore, documents and jewelry from Brownie Holmes who was the son of Dick Holmes who was present in the home of Julia Thomas on October 25, 1891 when Jacob Waltz died.

At the time of Jacob Waltz' death on October 25, 1891, Dick Holmes obtained the ore belonging to Jacob Waltz that was under his bed in a candle box at the time of his death. The ore was taken to Goldman's store in Phoenix, Arizona where it was assayed. I have seen the assay report on this ore and this assay report indicates that it was assayed at Goldman's store by Dick Holmes. The assay report further states that the ore assayed at $110,000 a ton and that gold at that time was selling for $20.64 an ounce.

I have also seen shipping papers sending the ore to a jewelry company in San Francisco requesting that a matchbox, ring, tie pin and cuff links be made from the ore. I have seen the shipping papers shipping this jewelry back to Phoenix. I have also seen the matchbox and the ring made from this ore,

---

and I have seen the tie pin and the cuff links.

I was told by the individual who owns the assay report, jewelry and ore that this ore had been sent to the University of Arizona, School of Mines that has samples of gold ore from every known Arizona gold mine to see if the ore could be matched up with any known Arizona gold mine. I was further told by this individual that the University of Arizona, School of Mines had informed him that this ore that he had sent to them came from an unknown source.

The reason that I cannot name the individual who has the ore, jewelry and documents is that I promised that individual I would never divulge his name without his permission if he would show the ore to me which, as stated above, he did.

Further affiant sayeth not.

TOM KOLLENBORN

SUBSCRIBED AND SWORN to before me this __13th__ .day of __April__ , 1985.

Notary Public

My Commission Expires:
~~My Commission Expires Feb. 11, 1985~~

My Commission Expires Feb. 11, 1989

Epilogue

The reader has now been privy to all of the tales told through notes, diaries, interviews and speculation. When stated, the story as Sims told it was supposed to be direct quotes from Julia, also known as Helena. But, there are definite discrepancies between Sims' book and Jim Bark's notes and these two were the best of friends. Their collective efforts spanned, to quote Sims, "A half a lifetime." No two men ever agree on anything—friends or not. Also, the newsman didn't write his book until after Bark's death and at that time Sims Ely was an old man. Was Sims confused at that time? Had he decided the record should reflect only his truth? Or, should we conclude that the story is basically true with some differences which really don't matter?

Even the most casual reader would have to admit the story is one of the great mysteries of all time. The elusive pot of gold remains hidden in the bosom of rocky crags protected by whatever natural force. One may discard any acceptance of evil spirits, mystical forces or angry gods, but no one can refute the facts—death stalks the mine.

Brownie never found it. He and his father seemed to have been destined to have been catalysts in an ongoing search one could offer them pity for the frustration they must have felt, but do they need it? Brownie spent a lifetime doing what most men only dream of doing. And in the end his life lasted 89 years. He had to have been healthy. Doing what he did took strength and an indomitable spirit. Men who live out-of-doors, enduring the hardships mother nature flings at them, are always tougher and usually perform without stress or disease.

Sims left a permanent record for posterity. Sims dedicated his book, "To the Memory of Jim Bark my lifelong partner in the Arizona Mountains." What greater tribute could a man pay anyone. What they had enjoyed together is unequalled in Arizona history. What an adventure it must have been.

235

Herman Petrasch (right) and a prospector friend beside Herman's Superstition camp, 1979.

Herman Petrasch lived to a ripe old age in a beautiful place where peace is the norm. One would wonder if the anger he felt for Rhinehardt ever subsided. Did he awake one morning to see the sun shimmering on the sheer precipices of the towering mountains; hear a coyote wailing its loneliness; feel the breeze wafting through the canyons under a palo verde while sniffing bacon cooking on an open fire? If he did, he surely must have decided he had found the treasure after all.

And, what of Jacob himself? The gods must have selected him and him alone to build the myth. Perhaps, because he never used the gold for anything other than surviving or helping a friend, he was allowed to keep it—that is, until he decided to tell someone where it was. Did some great force sardonically create the mystery to affect men's fates?

Tom Kollenborn, who first learned the legend from his father, became intrigued by the mystique of the mountains. He will be remembered as the man who researched the truth. The Superstition Museum which opened in 1989 reflects his diligence.

The picture of Tom riding his horse, Crow, trailed by his ever-faithful dog, Duke, is known to many in Arizona. He has been called friend to all who search for the mine or otherwise need help in the Superstitions.

In 1988 Kollenborn received a Fulbright fellowship to study in Israel; accepted invitations to speak at Harvard University and the British Parliament plus many other honors because of his quest. This dedicated man refused many lucrative jobs elsewhere just so he could remain close to his beloved mountains. His knowledge of the place, its people, the mine and the myths fills his life—making him, without a doubt, the world's leading authority on that subject.

Tom personally escorted John Denver, Jerry Lewis, Dean Martin, Aldo Ray and John Schneider into the range on different occasions. Former President Ronald Reagan made his Death Valley Days series just over the hill and John Wayne had a ranch there. The land retains its power. People travel from all over the world to see it firsthand.

Attorney General Bob Corbin and Tom Kollenborn continue the saga initiated by Bark and Ely. Kollenborn has been seeking the mine since he was a boy, while Corbin started his search in 1957. Their friendship spans over two decades. They've shared not only the excitement of the hunt, but also, the abject pleasure of riding alone through desolate, forbidding canyons and sleeping out under the stars. Their adventure has been an enviable one, indeed.

Now, because of Walter Gassler, the legend goes on. Eleven people listed in this book are known to have found it; all died untimely deaths. If one counts the Spanish, Mexicans and Apaches, the list grows longer—and adding the unsolved murders which have occurred since the 1800s further increases the tragedy. So many lost their lives, yet even today no one actually has any gold to speak of.

One can only speculate upon the next unfortunate soul who will locate the Lost Dutchman Gold Mine. Will the curse claim that life or will it lay forever unclaimed as a part of the illustrious lore of the great American West?

HELEN CORBIN

❑ **THE CURSE OF THE DUTCHMAN'S GOLD** – The top-selling book on the Lost Dutchman's Mine which includes maps, documents and evidence proving the existence of this cryptic lost treasure...............................**$14.95**

❑ **KING OF THE ICE** – The life story of an Alaskan homesteader whose heroics in the bush are legend. Don Johnson became a mentor to the Inuit Eskimos near the Arctic Circle and the Aleuts on the Aleutian chain. A true adventure; a must read. **$12.95**

❑ **SENNER'S GOLD** – A diary found in an attic trunk revealed Al Senner's true story about the 1,000 pounds of stolen gold, where he hid it in the Arizona Territory and a skeleton in a shallow grave. Another true Superstition Mountain lost treasure. **$12.95**

❑ **TREASURE AT BATTERY POINT** – An infamous island lighthouse, just off Crescent City, California, becomes the setting for a page-turning thriller surrounding an apocalyptic search for sunken gold amid a dangerous love triangle. **$14.95**

Pro-Mack South
(480) 983-3484 FAX (480) 983-3279 or 800-722-6463
940 West Apache Trail - Apache Junction, AZ 85220
E-Mail: promack@phoenix.quik.com

Please send me the Helen Corbin books I have checked above. I am enclosing $_____ (please add $2.50 for each book to cover postage and handling in the U.S.). Send check or money order – no cash or C.O.D.s.

Mʀ./Mѕ.: _____

Aᴅᴅʀᴇѕѕ: _____

Cɪᴛʏ/Sᴛᴀᴛᴇ: _____ Zɪᴘ: _____

Please allow two to four weeks for delivery.
Prices and availability subject to change without notice.